Old Roads & Pannierways in
N·O·R·T·H E·A·S·T Y·O·R·K·S·H·I·R·E

Raymond H. Hayes, M.B.E., F.S.A.

© North York Moors National Park 1988 ISBN 0 907480 20 9

Raymond H. Hayes, M.B.E., F.S.A.

Whose generosity and enthusiasm has inspired many others to pursue an interest in local history and archaeology.

Photograph by courtesy of Yorkshire Evening Press.

ACKNOWLEDGEMENTS

I have wanted to publish the information on this subject for a long time. After the publication of *A History of Helmsley, Rievaulx and District* in 1963 (the author and John McDonnell were the main contributors to the two chapters covering Roads and Communications, V and XIV), it was stated that the Helmsley Group, later the Helmsley Archaeological Society, hoped to initiate a detailed survey of the medieval road system of North East Yorkshire. Notice of this was sent to the Yorkshire Archaeologial Society and to the Scarborough and Whitby Societies. The response was very limited. Only the Scarborough Society replied and two of their members, The Misses Horseman and Haigh, offered to undertake field work in the Robin Hood's Bay - Whitby area. John McDonnell the editor typed out some of my notes and other material he had collected, but the project was postponed and the Helmsley Group instead concentrated on the launch of *The Ryedale Historian*.

The re-printing of J.T. Sewell's book on Medieval Roads south and south-west of Whitby, was undertaken by the Whitby Literary & Philosophical Society in 1971 with a few revisions by Mr R.F. Moore. The text which is very informative on that area was much as in 1923, although there were no maps. See Appendix H.

In 1982 Bill Breakell then living at Castleton produced a pamphlet *Stone Causeways of the North York Moors* (1). This was useful but did not cover many of the causeways.

I wish to record my appreciation and thanks to John McDonnell for checking my manuscript and especially for his notes on bridges, and to Patrick Sutor of the National Park Office for much time and patience in revising the text.

Raymond Hayes

CONTENTS

Foreword 6

Introduction 7

Around Ralph Cross and Guisborough
Keldholme - Blakey Ridge - Ralph Cross 11
Ralph Cross - White Cross - Rosedale 14
Ralph Cross - Castleton - Danby Dale 15
Castleton - Lockwood Reservoir - Guisborough
   (incl. Quaker's Causeway) 16
Ralph Cross - Westerdale - Esklets 17
Westerdale - Percy Cross - Guisborough (Ernaldsti) 17
White Cross - Commondale - Guisborough and Skelton 18

Staithes and the Esk Valley
George Gap Causeway (Rosedale - Lealholm -
   Borrowby - Staithes) 19
Pannierman's Causeway (Castleton - Staithes) 20
Glaisdale Rigg - Egton 21
Lealholm - Stonegate 21
Egton Bridge - Egton - Westonby 22
Egton - Aislaby - Briggswath - Whitby 24
Grosmont - Sleights (Monks Trod) 25
Sleights - Iburndale - Sneaton (Sneaton Causeway or
   Monks Walk) 25

Around Whitby
Pickering - Whitby 27
Wade's Causeway (Amotherby - Cawthorn - Lease Rigg) 29
The Old Salt Road or Robin Hood's Bay Road (Saltergate -
   Robin Hood's Bay) 30
The Pannierman's Road or Causeway (Sil Howe - Hackness) ... 31
High Gate (Whitby - Hawkser - Robin Hood's Bay - Staintondale) ... 32
Goathland Area 33
Whitby - Lythe - Barnby 34
West Barnby - Ugthorpe - Borrowby 35

Rosedale Area
Kirkbymoorside - Hutton le Hole - Rosedale 36
Rosedale 36
Rosedale - Hamer 37
Hamer - Glaisdale 37
Hamer - Egton (Yarlesgate) 39

North & West of Kirkbymoorside

Thurkilsti (Welburn - Skiplam - Bransdale Ridge -
Turkey Nab - Battersby) 41
Magna Via (Helmsley - Roppa - Bilsdale Moor) 43
Helmsley - Laskill - Carlton in Cleveland 44
Ingleby Greenhow area 44
Bilsdale and Raisdale 45
Waingate - Rudland Rigg Road (Kirkbymoorside - Fadmoor -
Rudland Rigg - Battersby Bank) 46
Farndale - Monket Bank - Bransdale 47
The Hambleton Street 48
High Street and Turngate (Lythe - Scaling - Commondale - Kildale) 51
North of Hawnby 52
Sperragate (West of Helmsley) 53

The Southern Fringe

Welburn - Harome - Sproxton area 54
Helmsley - Pickering - Scarborough 54
Lockton - Levisham 55
Rosedale - Spaunton - Normanby 55

Bridges

Bridges 58

Appendices

A	Types of early roads	62
B	Extracts from Medieval Charters Relating to Roads	63
C	Vehicles used on medieval roads	64
D	Goods and merchandise carried	65
E	Alum	66
F	Pack Horses in The North	68
G	Thomas Harwood	69
H	Joseph Sewell	70
J	'Sty' Roads	71
K	How much smuggling went on we shall never know!	73
L	Pannierway Guidestones	74

Notes and references 75

FOREWORD

Within the North York Moors National Park are some of the most interesting archaeological sites to be found in Britain. We are fortunate that so much survives - no doubt as a result of less intensive land use than in other areas. Pannierways are of particular interest (being found more extensively in North Yorkshire than in nearly any other locality) and formed a vital economic link across a wild and desolate area for many centuries. This communication network remains to be explored today and the paper contains a wealth of source material for the beginnings of such exploration.

Raymond Hayes has been in the forefront of archaeological research for many decades and his activities and publications have added considerably to our knowledge in this field. His deep interest in our local history is well known and his explorations on foot, bicycle and even as one of the first cross country skiers in the area have gained him an unrivalled insight into early life on the Moors.

Always eager to impart his findings to others, Raymond has prepared this paper using a combination of geographical and archaeological knowledge. The result is a document that will have interest both for students of history and also the growing numbers of moorland walkers.

I am delighted that the National Park Committee could help with the publication of this important work and especially that it should have been produced as our contribution to the Archaeological Day held in honour of Raymond Hayes and his work in October 1988.

D. C. Statham
National Park Officer

INTRODUCTION

In this report I have tried to describe the roads, tracks and pannier trods making up the medieval road system of North East Yorkshire, based on documentary and economic as well as topographical and archaeological evidence. I have tried to cover most of them even though many have been incorporated into modern roads. The origin of most of them is uncertain, and where there is firm evidence it points to post-medieval rather than earlier dates.

To follow these old trackways, especially the ridgeways, gives a unique insight into the toils and difficulties of travel in the middle ages. They quickly become muddy and, in winter, snow bound. There were few guide stones until after 1711 (when the Justices at Northallerton ordered Guide Posts to be erected at crossways throughout the North Riding, see Appendix G), no adequate maps and few travellers carried a compass. Even as late as 1927 I once asked the way of a dalesman who said "Ther's a stoup up there, he'll tell ya weer ta gan but dean't ask him ony questions coss he's deaf and dumb".

The oldest routes across the moors were almost certainly ridgeways following the high ground between the dales such as Blakey Rigg and Rudland Rigg. They usually kept on firm ground avoiding bogs or rocky ground. On slopes they tended to form hollow-ways. These were narrow and in winter the sides collapsed blocking the track, or they were blocked by snow. Hence the tendency was to try to avoid bad sections by using alternative ridges so forming parallel hollow-ways as found on the Thurkilsti on Skiplam Ridge or north of Spaunton and Lastingham.

However, other trackways existed. The footpath from Barmoor north of Hutton le Hole to Gillamoor by Grouse Hall has bronze age burial mounds on its sides. Another large stony mound at SE 689905 lies only a few metres east of the River Dove near Grouse Hall. The fields near Gillamoor Mill have produced worked flints and two flint and stone axes. So there must have been a clearing through the forest here at that period.

Not until Roman times was a well paved causeway constructed: Wades Causeway, parts of which remain between Stape and Lease Rigg (p29).

But pannier transport did not require a metalled road in early times. In dry weather the pack animals could follow any reasonable track. Even large waggons laden with turf or coal could take short cuts over the open moor and I remember seeing one following the ridge between Hutton and Loskey Becks to Thorgill in 1916. On the limestone hills it was possible to drive light carts almost anywhere. This is the area where several chariot burials are found, but we have no evidence the owners ever made regular roads.

Breakell says the horses were usually Chapman Horses, Jaggers (Jaegar - German Hunter ponies) and Gals (Galloways). The latter and the Chapmans were both noted for their hard feet; sure footed and vital on the narrow steep tracks of the moors. They were rarely higher than 14 hands (4ft 10ins) as it would have been extremely difficult to load anything higher. In some parts of the country the packhorses with long backs were held in high esteem but on the North York Moors shorter backs would have been preferred for the heavy loads, coal, iron and stone.

He says this weight-carrying speedy horse, full of stamina was a product of the monasteries, Whitby, Guisborough & Rievaulx, who held a virtual monopoly on non-military horse breeding in the area for three centuries before the reformation, although documentary evidence is lacking. The horses of Rievaulx Abbey carried over 3 cwt of wool on their journey from woolhouse to harbour. Whitby Abbey had over sixty packhorses in 1394, largely concerned with their fisheries.

The various loads transported by packhorse required different types of panniers and other ways of attaching goods. Usually a pair of wicker baskets (known as wackers, bannisters or hampers) sufficed. Variations included 'Hottes', special baskets with hinged bottoms through which a load of coal, charcoal, stone or turf could be dropped. An alternative method of carrying coal was in a long sack or poke slung over the saddle or pannel more like a pad than a saddle: the wooden framework or tree not being used. A load weighing up to 4 cwt (200 kg) could be carried in this way, enabling 7 or 8 tons of coal to be transported by each packhorse track. Loads such as cloth could be strapped to the back of the horse by a 'Wanter', a leather girth band with a long rope. Breakell has sketches of the various panniers (2, and also see Appendix C).

Trains of up to 40 pack ponies on narrow causeways could cause chaos; hence the leading pony wore a bell collar to give warning of its approach. It was said on fine still days they could be heard for miles (Plate 20).

We have several references to medieval roads in the Ryedale Charters (see Appendix B). In his excellent book *The Medieval Foundation* (3), Sir Arthur Bryant says "Bridging the uncultivated wild between England's villages and little towns ran the roads trodden by growing numbers of men and horses.

The metalled highways with which Rome had spanned the country had long become a ghostly network, their paved surfaces defaced and broken by quarrying and deflected to serve local needs. The medieval road did not run straight from city to city. It meandered round field, park and pale, respecting a thousand local 'liberties' and quirks of history. It was merely a grassy trackway for horses, carts, cattle and sheep. It was not so much a road as a route over which travellers had a right to pass. The proprietors along its course were under obligation to keep it open. No-one might raise a fence across it, or dung heaps, or use it for quarrying stone and gravel - such encroachments were subject to fines. In winter the soft roads become quagmires, in summer a maze of hard-baked hoof holes. So much of the countryside was waste it was easy to make a detour across adjoining land. This created a multiplicity of tracks and made it easy to lose the way".

Sewell has an interesting quote from the North Riding Records of the time of Elizabeth I on the state of medieval roads. "Now to speak of our common high waies .... you shall understand that in the clay or cledge soil they are often very deepe and troublesome in the winter halfe .... all sorts of people do imploie their travell (labour) for six daies in summer upon the same .... the intent of the statute is verie profitable for the reparations of the decaied places, yet the rich do so cancell their portions and the poor so loiter in their labour, that of all the six scarcelie two good daies work are performed. The streets often do grow to be too much more gulled than before .... Of the dailie encroaching of the covetous upon the high waies I speak not .... roads 50 feet broad according to law are brought down to 12 or 20 ft. and 12 feet to 6 feet."

There is a tale of a miller who, wanting clay for his mill, took it from the middle of the public road. In the morning a journeyman tailor and his ass were found drowned in the hole. The local magistrate dismissed the case, saying 'where else could the miller get his clay?' (4).

John Rushton sends a note from the published quarter sessions record for July 1654. A presentment for the owners or occupiers of Riseborough Hagg (SE 757834) for not repairing a highway extending from High Close unto Wrelton Cliff. This is now a narrow lane called Cliff Lane, little used except by gipsies. It crosses Street Lane at the north end of Riseborough Hill.

Celia Fiennes describes late or post-medieval roads in her Journeys (1685-98). "Carriage was almost always done by long strings of pack animals. The reason was from the narrowness of the roads between good lands but where it is hilly no carriages can pass.

In Devonshire the way were so narrow, horses and carriages cannot pass; they are forced to carry their corn on horses' backs with frames of wood like pannyers on either side loaded high and tied with cords (5).

From Kendall to Bowness, six miles through narrow lanes, there can be no carriages but narrow ones like little wheelbarrows. They also use horses with a sort of pannyer, some close, some open - strewn full of hay, turf, lime or dung and everything they use". She mentions "an abundance of horses all about Kendall with their burdens". Roger North said from Kendall "they could write letters to most trading towns and have answers by the packhorses with returns (time being allowed) as certain as the post".

Even as late as the 18th century travellers were advised to hire a guide between Pickering and Whitby. In 1712 it took a coach six days to go from London to Newcastle.

Horse sleds were in use from early times until the mid 20th century in the Dales, especially in time of snow and for leading hay and corn. Sleds also ran well on steep grassy slopes. In the hard winter of 1947 Harold Dobson of Hagg End, Farndale drove his horse sled to Kirkbymoorside market even when the road was blocked for ten weeks. He came down into Hagg Wood onto Hutton Road at Yoadwath Bank top. The latter section was the only difficult one.

Up to the late 1930s many dale roads had gates, as many as ten or more in five miles. These took time to open and shut especially in snow. The reason for this was the 'stint' of grazing between the farms where horses and cows were allowed to feed.

The ox-drawn waggon was used for heavy loads in Roman times and throughout the Middle Ages. It survived into the mid 19th century. As Canon Atkinson described on the road near Stonegate and Lealholm "I was no longer the sole traveller on this rugged lonely roadway; for here was a cavalcade such as I never before imagined, much less realized. What I met was a stone-waggon with a team, a 'draught' as we call it in North Yorkshire vernacular, of no less than twenty horses and oxen attached to it. They were drawing a huge block of freestone up the terribly steep bank which rises like a house roof on the eastern side of Stonegate Gill. At the foot of the bank, on the limited space available, there were standing four other waggons similarly loaded" (6). He estimated the load at five tons and says he had seen oxen used in ploughing, but never before had he seen such a spectacle as this on the high roads of England.

Paved trods were thought to be of monastic origin but there is no firm evidence for this. Roads occur in Medieval Charters though they do not mention paving or their materials. Post-medieval records do show useful evidence of the trod from Beck Hole to Goathland (p34) laid in 1715, and New Lane near Lealholm 1769. In many cases they were merely foot trods and described as such by T. Harwood the road surveyor of Glaisdale in the late 17th and early 18th centuries. Not far from his home two fields down towards the beck a gatepost is inscribed "THIS IS BUT A FOOTWAY. T.H. 1735". Harwood is described in Appendix G.

Canon Atkinson called paved causeways "old highways of the late medieval period often sunk in boggy places... within a mile of this house (Danby Vicarage) is where the old flagged causeway between all, or most, of Cleveland from Staithes to Redcar and Kirbymoorside.... used to run along the side of a steep hill 600 - 700 feet above sea level; from the nature of the subsoil and slow dribblings of the hillside gutters, the solid flags of the causey sank year by year. At the parish meeting on the spot, it was decided to do away with the old flags entirely and replace them with a good firm roadway, which was duly done... the first bit of modern road in the parish". (7)

A recent renovation of this type occurred in Danby village at Claymire Gate (p22), when flags were removed and the track tarred. There are many instances of this taking place around Lealholm and Eskdale. Improvements to roads and horse transport gradually ended the pannier ways, though the final blow to them came with the railways.

Sewell of Whitby in his book on Medieval Roads (8) - says:

"The writer well remembers being driven to Helmsley in 1868/9, where he saw the spacious market place occupied by a large drove of pit ponies, donkeys etc. Each beast carried two deep pannier baskets slung across the back, in this case filled with coal which they had brought from some Durham pit". He looked back on this scene as a picture of the style of traffic that passed along the pannierman's trods in ancient times. There were similar scenes at Castleton before the arrival of the railways (seen by Sewell) and at Kirkbymoorside. The late William Carter of Kirkbymoorside said he was at Fangdale Beck in Bilsdale with John Wood in the early years of this century, when a large drove of pannier ponies and donkeys passed to Spout House where they left coal and took packs of oats back to Cleveland or Durham. Much moor coal was carried this way.

Coal from moors north of Ampleforth was brought to Gilling East by pannier men from Bolton Bank, Agar's Bank and by the boundary west of Lodgefield Farm. It happened as late as the 20th century. (9)

At Guisborough, the railway came in the mid 19th century, to the fear and consternation of the old folks. It finished the old colliers. Willie Dickenson, in Belmangate, with his drove of fifty donkeys was the last of them. Two comrades, Willie Garbutt and John Patty, who had travelled together for years bringing fuel to the town, felt deeply the change that was coming. Said Willie, "What sall weah deaah noo, John, when there's neah coals to lead, and folks weant want sticks an torves fetching, when t'railway brings then plenty o coals, we sall ev nowt ti deahh? An beath us an oor 'ooses all starve ti deaath". "Whist, Willie", replied John, "deaant tack on like that, keep yer aart up man, and niiver heead the'll be summat fer us ti deeah, aal be bun, - mebbie they'll find us a job at' t' station - deant fret - t' trouble may'nt be as bad it leaaks". John kept up his courage and got employment at the station but Willie gave way to despair and died a broken-hearted man. (10)

AROUND RALPH CROSS AND GUISBOROUGH

KELDHOLME - BLAKEY RIDGE - RALPH CROSS

This important ridge road runs from its junction with the modern A170 at Keldholme, 166ft above sea level to 1400ft at Ralph Cross and on to Castleton. Keldholme corner (SE 710859) is the junction of four roads. Nearby is a footpath which might have been part of an old cobbled trackway leading to the site of a Cistercian nunnery known as Keldholme Priory (11). From Duna Lodge the road followed a narrow lane, formerly a deep hollow-way called Gray Lane or Bog Hall Lane. At its north end a Green Lane runs eastwards onto Appleton Common. The boundary of the priory land ran along this lane and the Spaunton Manor Boundary (boundary stone at SE 711869) still exists. The manor boundary is traditionally perambulated on the accession of a new Lord of the Manor and this was last done in 1986. The road to Hutton runs on the edge of Yapley Valley, by old quarries and remains of limekilns. The kiln is mentioned in the grant of land by King John in 1201 to the Prioriy. (12) From Halfway House Farm at Lickyatt Head (SE 709880) two parallel hollow-ways run on the east side of the present road, to Hutton Bank top. Much limestone was quarried here in the 18-20th centuries. The later road to Douthwaitedale ran by Westfield Farm under a set of whale jaws, now in the Ryedale Folk Museum. (13) For the old direct route from Kirkbymoorside via Yoadwath see page 36.

Descending the bank (called Yan Brow in the 17th century) the road passes through the village of Hutton le Hole and by the Ryedale Folk Museum. Here there were formerly three fords where the thirsty horses could drink, and two inns for the equally dry carters. From the village the road rises to the moor edge at 625ft accompanied by two hollow tracks, and others converge from the north west at Barmoor. Quarries, by now in sandstone, produced rather poor road metal and children were sent up to gather 'rubstones' for scouring the steps or hearths, a custom now discarded.

Just west of Barmoor at SE 698907, at the foot of Hutton Nab, are the three burial mounds mentioned on p7. They were dug by miners in the late 19th century and a cremation urn of mid bronze age found. It is in the Yorkshire Museum.

Farndale End road came in from the north-west at SE 696919. Several shallow hollows on the west side are marked 'old gravel pits' on the 6" OS map but they are probably for road metal. The Spaunton Manor boundary stones follow from Hangman Slack where the unlikely tale is told of a man who had stolen a sheep and tied its hind legs together and having put his head between them allowed the carcase to hang down his back. Coming to the stone, he sat down and placed the dead sheep to rest on top of the stone, but the carcase slipped over the far side and the man was literally hanged by the legs round his neck. This legend is told of several other 'hanging' stones all over the country.

At 775ft the old Kirkbymoorside road from Lowna converges from the south-west (Lund Road on the map, though called 'Ord Sandy Road' by locals.) It is deeply sunken with hollows on the sides. About 40 feet east of its junction with Blakey Ridge road side stands a good example of an 18th century guidestone (SE 693926) inscribed 'ROAD TO PICKRIN or MALTON,' with a hand pointing south. On the west side is: 'ROAD TO KIRBYMOORSIDE' (R.B. R.E. WEST). On the north side 'ROAD TO GISBOROUGH' (hand pointing to the sky). R.B. was possibly Richard Burton of Hutton. The stone was probably erected in 1712 by order of the justices at Northallerton. It stands on the side of a hollow-way 6ft deep and 8ft wide, with another two running parallel on the east. They all point to the junction of Lund Road. The present Hutton road from this point was a deep hollow track up to the early 20th century. The windings of the present road confirm its origin (Plate 1).

Another hollow track comes from Thunder Heads, Farndale to join the ridge way just north of the guide stone, and a track goes to Spaunton Lodge, a shooting house of 1770 still occupied by a gamekeeper.

The ridge road runs north over Pricket Thorn, through two deep cuttings often blocked by snow. (A pricket was a young deer). The next stone by the road is Saddle Stone - so called by its resemblance to a saddle. Just north is Stepin Turn - a sharp double bend in the road. The former Step Inn is now a sheep shelter surrounded by small pasture fields. Farndale tradition makes it the piece where 'they first stepped into the dale'. It was called 'Stebins' in the North Riding Records (14). John Stibbins was a Farndale poacher fined in 1334 AD.

450 yards south-east at SE 699937 lies a large medieval enclosure on both sides of Hutton Beck, a long vaccary or sheep or cattle fold (15). Hollow tracks lead to it from the south-east and north-west.

The ridge road attains over 1000ft and is fairly straight for 500 yards to the water troughs at SE 689954. These were restored in 1952 and have a constant flow of water. The old road is used as a lay-by.

Between this point and Stepin Turn the road crosses at right angles another old road coming from Farndale called Beggars' Track. It is shown on the 1856 OS map as running east from Duck House, Farndale (SE 683945) by Stepin Turn, crossing the dry ground at the head of Rudland Slack at SE698947, and over the narrow part of Jewel Mere. There is no track marked on the modern OS 1:25,000 sheet. The Beggar's Track ran east for about two miles and turned north-east by the Three Howes (tumuli) and descended into Rosedale by the present Bank Farm to Lane Head (now White Horse Inn). Near the Three Howes other tracks passed over the Hutton road to Ainhowe(Ana) Cross and followed the ridge by the Glass Holes and Abram's Hut (tumulus) down to High Askew and by lane and modern roads to Cropton and Appleton. The origin of the name is unknown. It could have been given to the travellers or pack-men of various types who used it in the 18-19th centuries. It is unpaved but a fairly deep hollow-way in parts, and is still traceable by these and later tracks.

At 1155ft on Low Blakey Moor the ridge road passes close to a series of quarry pits called Stonehaggs, thought to be old ironstone workings and previously thought to be a 'British settlement' of pit dwellings (16). Many stones taken from this area were used for road repairs, and it is likely this was why the pits were dug!

On the east is Pike Howe, a tumulus on the boundary line. Several tracks lead past it towards Sheriff's Pit, a 19th century ironstone mine that ceased to work about 1910 (17). Northward lie a large number of moor coal pits, now filled in but with conspicuous spoil heaps. They were worked in the late 18th century but the resulting coal was not very good quality and only used for lime burning (18).

The road crosses Sled Shoe Slack before rising to 1200ft above Little Blakey where the ridge is at its narrowest, only 200 yards wide. Here roads from both Farndale and Rosedale converge and in the 19th centuries the Rosedale Mineral Railway passed under it by the only bridge on its entire line of twenty miles (17). A small community of railwaymen lived here in cottages on the Rosedale side and a large lodging house stood close by the road at the bridge. From the junction a line went round Rosedale Head to the depots on the east side.

Branching on the Farndale side was a spur from an incline above the short lived Blakey Mines, 1876-95. Traces of the winding house were still visible in the 1980s. The earlier track from Farndale climbed Blakey Bank further north than the present road passing by Pannierman's Spring and Seaves (rushes) at SE 680991. There are no pannier flags visible here and the track may never have had paving. On the east a road from Millfield Bridge and Rosedale head climbs to the ridge. The boundary stones follow close to the west side of the road along with numerous coal pits and shallow quarries.

The Lion Inn at Blakey stands at 1300ft and must have been a welcome sight to wayfarers in the past, as it is at present to anyone caught in the severe blizzards of the moorland winters. In the 18th and 19th centuries up to 1930 it was considered a remote outpost. More cash was made by the landlords in mining moor coal at times. It was a calling house for fishmongers carrying fish from Staithes and Runswick to Kirkbymoorside and even York. Sewell mentions Thomas Wade in the early 19th century, who by changing horses at Ralph Cross was able to deliver fish at York the same day (19). Fish Willy Frank of Hutton le Hole traded in fish by changing horses at Blakey each journey and arriving at his shop the same day, a journey of twenty-five miles. The first mention of Blakey occurs in the Charter of Guisborough Priory in 1200. It is called Blakenhow or Blakehow, which simply means Black Howe, referring to the large tumulus that stands behind the inn, with a boundary stone on top. It has a deep hollow in the centre. No record of its excavation exists, but it could well be of the same age as Loose Howe on the opposite side of Rosedale, (p15) which is certainly Mid-Bronze Age about 12-1400 BC (20). The hollow on top was used for cockfighting in the 19th century or earlier.

Fred Johnson, landlord of the Inn with his father from 1915-39, said it had a Roman sign, and that they hung a bunch of green leaves or a bush outside after brewing. This was certainly a very old custom. Later owners had a sign by the road stating it dated back to 1553. I have not found any evidence of this, though there is a reference in Dugdale (21) stating that Edward III gave one toft and ten acres of land, in the moor of Blakeshowe in Farndale, Yorks, to the Crouched Friars for the building of an oratory, with other edifices for habitation, AD 1348. But Whitaker thinks this could be on the site of the present Farndale Church at the foot of Blakey Gill in Farndale (22).

Joe Ford (23) in 1944 wrote "Two hundred years ago or even less, the farmers in the neighbouring dales found a market for their spare corn, chiefly oats, at this wayside inn; also, bacon and hand woven goods were sold to commercial men, who at fixed dates, visited Blakey to buy these wares". There is a picture of a (1970) sheep sale at Blakey in Hartley and Ingilby's *Life in the Moorlands of North East Yorkshire* (24).

The ridge road was tarred in 1932 but only in the late 1930s did many people have cars to drive over the moors. The inn was bought for £300 by Fred Middleton in 1939. It changed hands for much larger sums later.

Continuing north along Blakey Rigg, a branch from Jackson's Road runs round the head of Blakey Gill, fording the stream above the waterfall, and joins the main ridge road above the howe. Jackson's Road is marked as a track climbing steeply from Head House, Farndale. The farm is mentioned in a Farndale Lay Subsidy of 1327 with Ralph & John del Hed as tenants. A deep hollow-way on the slope divides in two; later crossed by the mineral railway. It is very clear on two air photos (25), and does not appear to continue east of the Castleton road. Nothing is known of Jackson; possibly a tenant in the mid 19th century who used it for leading turf or stone. There is another Jackson's Bank to the north side of the Cleveland Hills (p43).

The deep cutting at 1315ft is a snow trap; in the severe winters of 1947 and 1963 this section north to Ralph's Cross was blocked for weeks. A stone just north at NZ SE 679999, is inscribed ROSEDALE ROAD NORTH; another about a mile distant is F.R. END (Plate 2). This was described by a writer in the 'Dalesman' as a mystery stone and he assumed someone called Fred Roe met his end in a blizzard here as in the Old Ralph legend! There is nothing mysterious about it, merely marking the stint for the 19th century roadmen from Farndale and Rosedale to work between the two stones. A more famous stone, Margery Bradley, stands at almost 1400ft (NZ 675013). This was called 'my boundary towards Cleveland' by an early medieval lord. It marks the boundary of three lordships and the track now used as the Lyke Wake Walk passes by it. A massive block of moorland sandstone 5ft high 3ft wide at the base, it could well be prehistoric; it is Merey Bradley in one document - possibly from mere, meaning boundary. The hollow track coming from Rosedale Head and Fat Betty cuts the corner off towards it and continues to Esklets and Westerdale head.

The Spaunton Manor boundary turns east to Seven Stones and the stream in Rosedale Head. The ridge road now rises to 1400ft at Young Ralph Cross (NZ 678023, Crucem Rudulphi), AD 1200, probably from the Old Norse 'Ralpa', meaning a heap (of stones). The cross may be much more recent than its counterpart Old Ralph which stands 300 yards to the west at NZ 676020, at just over 1400ft the highest point on the ridge. No deep hollow track is visible near it. One wonders if it was removed from the original site when the taller cross was erected. The old custom of leaving a coin or food on top has persisted and led to its downfall by a man who rushed to climb on to it for the cash, causing it to break into three pieces. Restored in 1941, it was blown down by a great gale in November of the same year and in 1985 it was deliberately pulled down by a rope attached to a motor car or lorry. Legend says it was erected where a local man called Ralph perished in a blizzard, and Crosland told another story of it in his delightful book *Yorkshire Treasure* (26) this time of its monastic origin, the outcome of a dispute between the nuns of Rosedale and Baysdale Priories. It certainly marks four main roads of medieval or earlier origin. From it the coast can be seen through gaps in the high cliffs (Plate 3).

To the north-west runs the fine ridge road into Westerdale down Ledging Hill. This road goes down through the village and crosses the Esk over Hunter's Sty Bridge (p17).

From Ralph Cross another high-level road turns eastwards by White Cross or Fat Betty as it is usually called, owing to the massive base without a shaft and a wheel-head type cross on top. Possibly an early Norman monument, the only wheel-head on the moors, it marks the old hollow track from Margery Stone towards the Western Howes (Bronze Age relics found in them by Canon Atkinson, 27). Here the boundary stones follow an old track due north to Stone Rook Hill, another tumulus dug by the Canon (also 27).

It has by now joined the main ridge road which traverses Castleton Rigg, a narrow edge between Westerdale and Danby. At NZ 683039 the ancient track was blocked by a cross-ridge dike, High Stone Dike which must have guarded the road in the Bronze Age, probably with a gate. The rampart is still impressive, 6-8ft high and 18ft wide, with upright stones set on it and a ditch on the south side, 10ft wide. The ridge is only 120 yards wide at this point. Half a mile north is another bank astride a somewhat wider ridge. There are crags on the east side but on the west only a steep slope. Between the dikes were many stony mounds, once though to be burial cairns, but more likely clearance for cultivation. The banks were probably intended to stop animals eating the crops rather than a defence against invaders. On the east and west sides there may have been a palisade.

An old track into Danby Dale joins the Quaker's Way at NZ 688049 and runs on the west side of the dale above Stormy Hall to Nook House, and Honey Bee Nest. It is also known as the Pannierman's Track. It was most likely much earlier than the Quakers, but used by them to travel to their Guisborough Meeting. The paved trod above Aysdale Gate (p16), was part of this route (28).

RALPH CROSS - WHITE CROSS - ROSEDALE

Branching from the Hutton-Castleton Road just south of Ralph Cross, and heading south-east this road is one of the highest on the North York Moors. It winds round Rosedale Head passing several old coal pits by Fat Betty, also known as White Cross (not to be confused with that near Commondale). It is, as already mentioned, a wheel-head type (29). It is painted white to mark the boundary, according to a local wag to 'show the grouse which side they belong'. This section is high - over 1400ft and often blocked by snow. It is mentioned as a road by 1223 in the Guisborough Charter. Before the Fryup road junction the remains of Botton Cross lie towards the head of Danby High Moor at 1387 feet. Only the base stone is left. Botton is old Norse for a hollow. A vast expanse of moorland and part of the coast can be seen with Roseberry Topping to the west.

The road passes close to Loose Howe (NZ 703008), a famous tumulus excavated by Billingham W.E.A. Group under the direction of Mrs. H.W. Elgee in 1937 (20). The primary burial was in a massive oak tree-trunk coffin shaped like a boat or dug-out canoe with a cover. It contained the scanty remains of an inhumation with a bronze dagger laid on hazel branches. Higher in the mound was a later burial, cremated bones in a broken urn with another bronze dagger and a bronze pin, also a small cup-like vessel of uncertain use, all mid to early Bronze Age, 1400 BC or earlier. The mound was of turf cased over with stone and the oak coffin shaped like a boat or canoe points to a very early burial custom 1500 years before the Sutton Hoo boat burial of early Saxon times. The moors were then afforested with much hazel in the clearings, as proved by Professor Dimbleby in 1961 (30).

Just east of Loose Howe the road crosses the line of George Gap Causeway (p19) and parts of Rosedale come into view. Our road turns along the side of Northdale. This little valley once had twelve to fourteen small holdings, now reduced to one large and one smaller farm. Some of the ruins have remains of crucks and saltboxes. There are two stretches of paved trod near Northdale Farm. Clough Dike Head is passed (Clough is uncommon in N.E. Yorks though used in the Pennines and West Yorks - it denoted a ravine or valley.). The descent into Rosedale is by the Knott, a sharp ridge by Abbey Heads and Bell End.

RALPH CROSS - CASTLETON - DANBY DALE

The main road continues north past Brown Hill. The name is probably derived from the Celtic Bron meaning 'breast' (see Elgee, 31) and there are several other hills of this name in the North York Moors. On the side of the road is a strong spring filling a stone trough used in the days of the horse transport and still by picnic parties. On the east are two small fields, although intakes from the moor north-east of these are now destroyed. Gallow Howe (NZ 682074) was once an impressive cairn of stones with a walled cist 5ft by 3ft but is now destroyed. Atkinson could not find a burial in it (32). A lop-sided flint arrow head was found nearby in 1953 and pieces of urn near the road. On the north end of the rigg was an important junction of old roads called Shaw End by the locals. There is a massive block of stone inscribed Gallow Howe 1833 D (for Danby). Here the parish boundary turns west to the Esk south-west of Dibble Bridge. A trackway leads to Birkfield Bank from Westerdale Old Road. There in the fence of an intake by a quarry is an old milestone (NZ 679075). It is about 2ft 6in high, very weathered and divided into portions, a base, central block, and bevelled broken top. It looks suspiciously like a re-used Roman Altar. Beehive type quernstones were found nearby. The stone is inscribed TO STOXLAY (NE) TO WHITBY (NW) with crude hand. TO KIRBY (SW) and in the SE panel possibly, 1797. (Fig 1)

Joe Ford (23) describes the Stokesley road as crossing Crown End, a mile west of the above site. It must have followed the deep hollow to the Esk Ford. The alternative route is by Dibble Bridge via Hare Slack. Parallel roads ran to Westerdale on a shelf below this stone. The main Castleton rigg road follows through the town winding by Castle Hill, where it is said to run in the filled up moat of the castle. It takes sharp bends to cross the Esk near the site of the old Bow Bridge, built 1175-85 but destroyed 1873. Canon Atkinson (in Forty Years, 33) has a sketch of the old bridge which shows a paved trod crossing the ford east of the bridge (NZ 685084).

East of the ridge road is Danby Dale. There is much paved trod along its western side though less on the east side. There is also good paving near the church (NZ 697063).

CASTLETON - LOCKWOOD RESERVOIR - GUISBOROUGH (including QUAKERS CAUSEWAY)

The present road passes north of Bow Bridge, Castleton and Conn House (34), where a beehive quern was found, past several old quarries climbing to Howl Dike Head, where, about 800ft west on a bracken covered ledge, is a small square embanked enclosure (NZ 678093) near Pinnican Hill possibly from Celtic 'pen', meaning hill, described by Elgee (35), as about 130 by 140ft. He dug part of it without finding any clue to its origin. Rowland Close and the author had four hours there and found that the south ditch was full of burnt stones at the angle but few in the other ditches. One small piece of base may have come from an Iron Age, or native Roman pot. There were three pits just outside the enclosure full of burnt stones; also the bedrock was heavily burnt. We thought the pits were for parching grain; querns found in the vicinity point to milling operations.

The road north rises to 800ft and higher up the hill passes five tumuli, those on the east called 'Three Howes' (dug by Atkinson). There are parallel hollow-ways east of the modern road. At White Cross, (NZ 679108), five tracks merge. Ton or Turn Gate is crossed at right angles (see p51).

A raised and cambered road runs directly to Dimmingdale Farm; it may be recent. At NZ 686118 on a ridge north-north-west of the farm, on Moorsholm High Moor, is a remarkable embanked oval enclosure, 91 by 79ft. It may well be an enclosed cremation cemetery (36).

From White Cross (a shaft in a plain socket) the present road rises to 925ft on (another) Brown Hill (see p15). In a bog to the east - Loggerheads Hole, the 6ins OS map marks "Ancient Bell found before1850". At Tod Howe (Tod is Norse for Fox, NZ 669118) is an old broken way-marker, with D - for DANBY, and G - for Guisborough; many hollow-ways converge here. The modern road runs due north to Lockwood Beck (reservoir). The old track goes instead past the Black Howes (NZ 665125) with multiple burials, cremations in Bronze Age urns. Several hollow tracks turn north-wards to Lockwood Beck head.

The route from White Cross to Aysdale Gate is known as The Quakers' Causeway and at NZ 663127 a paved trod retains its flags, some 3-4ft in length, 2-2ft 6ins wide. They are not deeply worn nor do they show repairs. Many old sunken tracks curve west above Skelton Old Peat Holes. At NZ 655141, south-east of Wood Hill, the paving vanishes in a bog. No trace of the raised ridge or ditches mark its line.

The track runs east of Wood Hill Gill and vanishes into a quarry at Aysdale Gate. Presumably it continued via Charltons to Guisborough three miles distant. Sewell (37) says "if we may judge from the substantial stonepath that starts from near Haydale (presumably Aysdale) Gate in the neighbourhood of the Priory, and crosses the wet moor above Lockwood Reservoir, this path would be the connection between Guisborough and Commondale, and from thence to Baysdale Priory". This is very doubtful; the most direct route from Baysdale would be via Kildale or Little Kildale by the Ernaldsti (see p17) and Percy Rigg to Rothergate. Sewell also says "this trod across the moors from Haydale Gate, is quite erroneously spoken of as the 'Quaker's Path'; the path made by the Quakers is a much more simple way that connects Rosedale and Danby Dale. It runs along the west side of the latter, descending at the St Helena Farm into the dale" (37, and see p). But Dr. Elgee, says "it is so named because it was much used by the followers of Fox, in travelling from Guisborough to Castleton in the early 18th century" (38). (The Quakers had a meeting house at Guisborough.)

RALPH CROSS - WESTERDALE - ESKLETS

Another ridge road branches off theBlakey road at Ralph's Cross (p14). It runs straight in a north-north-west direction for almost two miles, passing six quarries, including also Farndale Quarry and Westerdale Quarry, near to an unsuccessful oil bore hole sunk in 1970. The ridge narrows to 100 yards at Top End, then falls rapidly to Westerdale village street. Here paving stones are visible on the west side at NZ 664057, winding down the hill to Hunter's Sty bridge NZ 663062, much restored in 1878 (39). (Plate 4)

On the east side of the village a Templars' Preceptory was founded in 1203 and about 100 years later they were suppressed (1301). Very little is known of the Westerdale House. Even the site is doubtful; Town Farm may be the locality (40). This was at the junction of four tracks just east of the village Christy Cross, figured by Young (41); it stood on a pedestal 2ft 4ins square and had a shaft almost 6ft high, with an unusual triangular holed head. It has now gone, but the location is marked on the map. Broadgate road south from this junction led to iron smelting workings and slag heaps. A paved trod runs from NZ 671052 eastward down to the stream, Tower Beck, at a place named Cock Bannock, which is surely a Celtic place name survival meaning "Cairn-Hill".

West of the village at a point marked 'PITS' on the 6 inch OS map at NZ 664056 are the ancient ironstone workings called Sub-Ref Holes in the Guisborough Charter of the 13-14th century. A paved trod leads by them continuing south-west past Riddings Farm (NZ 659048) as far as Daleside Farm, on the side of the present road. An old hollow-way leaves this road further back, at NZ 665053. It goes across Tor Hill to a paved ford across Clough Gill at Hunter's Wath (NZ 661034). This is in Wood Dale, called Wolf Dale in the 12th century. The path continues as a cambered and paved ridge passing east of Piethorn (ruin at NZ 657027) and thence to Esklets. This was the site of a monastic grange of Rievaulx, (42). It must have always been a bleak outpost 800 to 1000ft above the sea and facing north. Yet querns of Roman type have been found up there. A track leads up to the col between Westerdale and Farndale.

WESTERDALE - PERCY CROSS - GUISBOROUGH (ERNALDSTI)

Going north-west from Hunter's Sty Bridge, Westerdale, a paved trod is still visible in part on a raised bank east of the present road for 300 yards towards the moor gate. No trace remains on Westerdale Moor where a later road ran from the Stocking Farm (called John Breckon road). On the slope to Hob Hole at 750ft is a small wailed enclosure at NZ 653072 called Gin Garth locally and said to be the resort of smugglers and drinking parties from places as distant as Kirkbymoorside! (See Appendix K). Up to 1960 the remains of a thatched two-bay house survived with what might have been a large malting and still kiln at one end and remains of an earlier iron bloomery (smelting furnace). Rowland Close found post-medieval pottery here including a loving cup, and incorporated in the outer wall on the north-east is a shaft and base named Stokesley Cross. A short distance to the south is a stone inscribed WESTERDALE ROAD EAST 1735.

Further south in a stony outcrop is the site of Shinnera Cross (NZ 650066) named on the Duncombe Park Estate Map of 1829 (43). A large number of tracks curve up from Baysdale Beck where Rowland Close found medieval iron working (44). These tracks show on 1946 RAF photos and may be part of the road known as The Smuggler's Track by Brandy Bridge, near the present ford at Hob Hole and Gin Garth at NZ 653072, 300 yards south. The present road from Hob Hole climbs steeply to Kempswithen, at 900ft the scene of a failed attempt to reclaim boggy moor about 1770. Walls and gateposts remain. The old name Hassock Mire could could have told them this was unsuitable ground.

On 900ft on Kildale Moor a ring-cairn was dug by Rowland Close. It had a cremation with flints in the centre. A steep descent to West House and the railway line passes a deep bog, Peat Carr. At the junction with the Commondale-Kildale road is Crag Bank where Romano-British occupation was found in 1975 (45). In fact there are several sites of this period in the Kildale Gap. The direct route north goes up Percy Rigg to Hutton Gate near Guisborough and is called Ernaldsti, after Ernald de Percy, Lord of Kildale. There is also a spur direct from Kildale to Great Ayton Moor. A large pre-historic settlement site lies on the south-west slope of Percy Rigg at NZ 620110, with fields, walling and hut sites, all very ruinous and on the farm at the south end of the rigg, bee-hive type querns (46). This site continues up to yet another Brown Hill, 916ft (see p15).

About 300 yards south of Percy Cross is a group of five round stone-based huts at NZ 610116 excavated by Rowland Close in 1961-64 and fenced by National Park staff. They remain a memorial to this energetic archaeologist. They produced native pottery of the late Iron Age to Roman period, evidence of grain cultivation and querns both saddle and rotary types (47). A hollow-way 4 feet wide and 1ft 6ins deep, crosses a ditch on the north-west, which had been filled with stones from the ruined huts to make a crossing place. Sled tracks 2ft 6ins apart went over hut 'D'. Percy Cross stood on a tumulus under a ruined wall. Woodwark shows it as having a short, possibly broken shaft and is inscribed RC TC 1856 (48). The shaft has now gone and the socket lies further to the south. It is mentioned in 1642, but has probably been replaced since then. The howe was excavated by R.S. Close. It contained a stone cist with a few cremated bones and one jet bead, of late Bronze Age type: More evidence of the early use of the ridge road.

The road climbs to 1000ft at Black Nab descending to Hutton Gate and Low Cross, the site of a forerunner of Baysdale priory. It is a very fine example of a ridge road with wonderful views of Cleveland all the way from Ralph Cross and plenty of evidence of its early origin.

WHITE CROSS - COMMONDALE - GUISBOROUGH AND SKELTON

Leading west from White Cross (p16) over Sand Hill intake a line of flags curves down into Commondale village just south of the school and close by the Methodist Chapel (NZ 662105). They may have continued by Potter's Side Lane to a guide stone west of Thunderbush. Near the latter farm at Whitley Bridge (NZ 653107) there is a good section recently uncovered going north-west to a brigstone of two parallel slabs over the beck. On the south-east side of the beck it appears to cut through the large enclosure bank of the North Ings earthwork (49). This portion is mentioned by Brown (50). There is little trace of it on the line of the present footpath by Hob On The Hill (NZ 646125), but the remarkable bank set with upright stones survives in parts; mentioned by Elgee (51) as a possible defensive work. The present track goes north to Hob Cross and Tidkinhow Head (NZ 645134). North of this point, in Tidkinhow Intake another length of paving remains at NZ 647134-5. The footpath turns east on the edge of the wood and the line of the trod may have been removed by Slape Wath Mine.

For the valley route from Commondale to Kildale and beyond see p52.

A medieval record of the 14-15th centuries (52) mentions a road near the line of the present Guisborough-Whitby A 171. It passes near Kateridden (at NZ 672147, south of Stanghow, and is Old Norse for "Kati's Clearing"). It continued to Le Haunes (now Avens House) at NZ 696128, across Skate Beck (Skaytebec in the 14th century) to the Harlow Bush boundary stone at NZ 717118 (Lardenthorn in the 14th century). In the perambulation of the Danby Forest boundary in 1666 this line is called Street.

STAITHES AND THE ESK VALLEY
GEORGE GAP CAUSEWAY
(ROSEDALE - LEALHOLM - BORROWBY - STAITHES)

This was probably the longest line of paved pannierway on the North York Moors but only portions remain. It leaves the main Blakey Rigg road (p13) near Little Blakey and continues eastwards across Rosedale by Hollin Bush. It passes Dale Head Farm (SE 696993) and is found climbing, steeply up the south-west side of Nab Scar.

On Nab Scar the paving is visible at SE 699004 where a standing stone (waymarker) 4ft high 10ins wide, has on its north-west side ROSDAL, on its north-east WHITBY. The causeway is 2ft 6ins wide and set on a raised bank 5ft wide and 2ft high. It continues under the turf as far as a similar stone (now fallen) at SE 006703. This is close to the modern Rosedale-Ralph Cross road but no paving stones remain here. I was told by the late Nick Peirson, a local keeper, that he was ordered by the estate to remove the paving where it ran near the modern road, because it might encourage walkers to follow it onto the grouse moor.

This is the origin of the gap on the north-east side, where it ran on the edge of Loose Howe, at 1400ft. (See p15). The ridge is visible all the way to Fryup with stones at intervals. A boundary stone inscribed CAUSEWAY STONE 1864 marks the Rosedale and Danby boundary, replacing an earlier one. On William Hill, coins of Elizabeth I have been picked up on its line. The route goes to the edge of Great Fryup where it descends a steep zigzag unpaved track into the dale. It follows the footpath in a plantation west of the beck where the paving stones appear again at Woodend (NZ 721034), and continues to Slidney Beck Farm. It then runs east of Fryup Hall to join another track called Long Causeway though the paving has gone. Turning north-east it passes Street (NZ 736047). Further north-east near Bainley Bank the paving is visible climbing up to Spring House (trough) at NZ 738052. At Hill Top, 775ft, it runs on the ridge to Shaw End where it joins the ridge road from Bluewath Beck. At one of these houses it once ran through the cross-passage. (There are four records of this happening elsewhere in North East Yorks, 53, see also p34).

The ridge road is called Yarlesgate and goes down to the cross roads at Lane End near Busco Beck Farm that were important in medieval and post medieval times. The Lane Head Guidestone at NZ 753060, pointed on top and about 5ft high has all four sides inscribed: - STATHES ROAD, WHITBY ROAD, KERBY ROAD and GISBORO ROAD. The paving is under a raised turf bank. (Plate 5, Fig 2)

Going east from the Lane Head Stone Busco Beck Farm lies at NZ 754060. Two flagged trods are found not far away: one coming down from Yarlesgate the other down Glaisdale Swang to a ford near Mull Hill, possibly from the ironstone workings. There is a paved path on the side of the present road to Glaisdale but this appears to follow the path by Bracken Hill to Lower Swang. Hangton Hill to the north is the Hanecheton of Domesday where Robert Bruce held two carucates later.

Dr. Elgee in his *Romans in Cleveland* (54) quotes from the Guisborough Cartulary "Flaga de Buscoe" (Birkercough, Birch Wood), dated 1200. The phrase was thought to be a vital clue in the dating of the flagged trods, indicating that the paving was in existence at that date. But does this name mean paving flags? Latham (55) gives FLAGA 1286-1306. FLAGGUS 1336, FLACCA 1270 from FLAG meaning reed, while the Oxford Dictionary defines FLAG, among other things, as a kind of coarse grass. One look at Birkscog or Busco shows an abundance of reeds or coarse grass, with plenty growing around the Lane Head stone. Yet this is still quoted to prove the existence of flagged trods in the Middle Ages or earlier.

The Staithes road followed down Lealholm Lane to the Esk Bridge. It climbed up to Lealholm Brow by Ellergate by a paved trod visible at NZ 765(6)080(3). The direct line north by Lealholm Rigg but west of Green Houses, Black Dike and Hardhill Slacks, is very boggy though there is a crossing at NZ 762102, still used by a modern path. At NZ 762098 is a turf bank curving round on the west side over 60ft long by 6ft 6in wide and 4ft high, shown on the 1850 OS map as a rectangle and called The Huts. This may be a shelter for travellers or possibly a sheep bield. This section is rather featureless and boggy; the nearest houses are at Green Houses, a quarter of a mile to the east (56). Near the Hardale Beck is a quarry, and others can be seen in Tranmire. The track follows the intake walls to 725ft where it divides, the northern route pointing towards Stepping Stone Hills where several hollow-ways converge near a circle - possibly the outline of a hut (57). The track is crossed by the Whitby-Guisborough Road on Standing Stone Rigg.

Continuing up to Roxby (Rousby in the 18-19th century) Low Moor, where there was a Cross Hill at High Roxby in 1850, at least eighteen deep hollow-ways run parallel to the present road. At NZ 761139 there was a ditched enclosure, ploughed out in 1972. This had internal ditches and an entrance on the north-east corner, and pottery from round hut sites inside was native ware of late Iron-Age to Roman period. Just north of this on the west of the road, four round huts of the same period were excavated by the Teesside Archaeological Society in 1973-81 (58). To the east of the road other enclosures called Soldier's Garths are most likely of the same period. A deep hollow-way runs close by them. It is certain this route to the coast was used over a very long period. From Borrowby the road goes downhill to Dalehouse Mill and thence to Staithes.

PANNIERMAN'S CAUSEWAY
(CASTLETON - STAITHES)

According to Sewell (59) the remains of a track to Staithes across from the Castleton moor through Rosedale Intake (NZ 706094) is one of the two routes called 'Pannierman's Causeway'. This unpaved track starts from Winsley Hill (NZ 700085), just north of Stangend the site of the cruck- house removed to the Ryedale Folk Museum in 1966, though there was little left of the original building (60). Elizabethan coins have been found on the track here. It climbs by Pannierman's Lane to Bellhouse Top though the main line goes to White Cross. The Sewell route crosses a ford over Ewe Crag Beck and slants north-eastwards towards Clitherbeck where much moor coal was obtained in the past. It reached its highest point on Elm Lodge (800ft). Where the Danby Beacon road crosses at NZ 719108 there are deep hollow-ways coming from the west to cross those of the causeway. In one hollow-way 12 ft 4 ins wide, a fallen guide-stone 4ft high lay. It is inscribed:

TON BY LA ?
CASIL WHIT STOX IX

The Beacon (225) stands at a fine viewpoint. The sea and the rear of the cliffs at Rockcliff and Boulby are visible. The causeway goes down Sandy Slack to Water Dittins on the Danby parish boundary. (Dittins was a cattle fence over a stream or bog). There are three or more hollow-ways with a broad balk between, and a raised bank but no stones visible. They may have sunk in the bog. It is cut by the unfinished railway workings for Paddy Waddell's Railway (61) and the modern road, at Waupley Bridge. Other tracks from Nean Howe Rigg (NZ 730102) join it here and others go north and north-east over Waupley Moor towards Staithes. The Whitby road probably went by Scaling and the Mickleby-Sandsend roads; it could also have followed the Ridge Lane from Scaling north to Staithes. There is very little of it paved but it was a fairly direct route from Castleton to the coast. Alternatively, the route from Waupley Moor past Grinkle Park to Easington, followed by a modern road, is mentioned in medieval documents.

GLAISDALE RIGG - EGTON

One of the roads from the Lane End Crossroads on Yarlesgate (p19) leads past Bracken Hill and through Glaisdale towards Egton and on to Whitby. Another line of paving goes down from Glaisdale Swang to Mill Hill.

The Egton road passes through the village of Glaisdale down to the Esk at Beggars Bridge, which was built for Thomas Ferris in 1619. He was a Hull lad who used to ford the River Esk to visit his girl friend, when floods did not stop him. Making his fortune he spent some of it on this bridge. A fine piece of paved causeway remains for half a mile following the south bank of the Esk, then climbs into Arncliffe Woods where it is 2ft 6ins to 3ft wide and 4-6ins thick. The stones are worn and dished in places, and some of it was damaged by tree-felling in 1962-3. Close to the Arncliffe Wood paved trod is a large stone called Kid Stone. Kids were bundles of fire wood and were set on this stone prior to placing on the pack horse. It was possibly joined by another track from Snowdon Nab and Delves (p39). (Plate 6)

From Delves at Egton Bridge there are three routes to Whitby. The first keeps in the valley by the river, from Egton Manor to Grosmont, the second goes by Egton Village, and the third by Key Green and Lease Rigg.

From the guide stone at Lawnsgate or Lane Head (NZ 754063) - to Whitby is the first of the three routes, from Egton Bridge to the toll road. Whether this was made in the years before the Fosters took the estate is doubtful, although it is a direct easy line, only 125ft OD all the way to 32 Grosmont, though liable to be flooded. However it is not shown on old maps, such as Knox's 1855 map.

It would have been possible to get to Key Green from Arncliffe Woods by following a line of footpaths to Key Green, but it is a difficult route. From Key Green, Lease Rigg Lane is the obvious route though it climbs at the east end and at the foot there is still the Esk to cross. But on this side of the Esk near Grosmont there was the Medieval Chapel of St. Lawrence at Chapel Garth (NZ 823053) where a jet crucifix was found in the early 19th century.

LEALHOLM - STONEGATE

From Ellergate above Lealholm the modern road goes to Stonegate (Staingate Side), which in the 13th century had a mill and ironworking. The track is beside the road and was paved a few years ago but now is only paved in parts.

From Stonegate the present road climbs steeply to Wilks Farm. Two footpaths leave the north side of the road, one at the above farm and another at Southgate Farm. Both converge after crossing a little valley by a ford, and continue north-east to the A171, Whitby-Guisborough Road. By following it a short way to the north-west the paved trod from Traveller's Rest Farm could be followed to Ugthorpe (p35). Further along the A171 past Ugthorpe Lodge at (NZ 784116), another path passes over Sheffield Moor by Newton Mulgrave Woods over to Ellerby after crossing High Street.

From Stonegate an old road runs west to Danby Beacon, which stands on a tumulus at NZ 737093, with commanding views in all directions.

Leavergate leaves the Danby Beacon road after the newly opened section of paving described in the next paragraph. It is given in the list of place names on the Danby Forest Boundary perambulation of 1660. It is a rough stony track used as a peat road. It probably started at Houlsyke, although this is not clear from the perambulation. Running west-north-west it leaves the Danby Beacon road near the remains of Stump Cross - probably the Roger Cross of the Danby boundary list (NZ 744094). Then it crosses Brown Rigg End and then a footpath from Houlsyke Danby which runs north-east across Roxby High Moor. There is a deep hollow-way at Scarth Nick (NZ 749097). The path skirts the head of Black Dike (to east) crossing Black Dike Moor between Good Goose Thorn (boundary stone at NZ 747109) and over Roxby Peat Holes. It crosses the north-east trackway from Staithes (p20) and follows the boundary line to Whin Rake east of Sail Howe, thence to Scaling Dam (where its route is now submerged by the reservoir) where it joined the Whitby-Guisborough Road. There is a northerly extension by Dodder Carr to Easington.

The Danby Beacon track leaves Stonegate at a guidepost at 670ft. It crosses Lealholm Rigg over the track to Staithes (p20) past a group of tumuli, and Rawland Howe (at NZ 754093), 34ft diameter, just north of Oakley Walls, where a burial in a stone cist was ploughed up in 1946 (62). A good section of paved causeway has been uncovered here by the National Park Department using Manpower Services Commission labour. The stones run eastwards from the curve south-east of the Oakley Walls road to Lealholm Brow. They continue to the ridge by a boundary stone at NZ 765087, inscribed J.H. 1869 and 5ft high and 10ins thick. The flags of the causeway are 3ft 8ins wide and 4ins thick. It is exposed for about 600 yards to a shallow gulley where it has sunk or been removed. The direction taken would lead east to Stonegate Mill and on to tracks to Wilks Rigg. (Plate 7)

At Brown Rigg Howe, (NZ 745094) Canon Atkinson dug into a conical stony cairn, finding a cremation with an axe head of basalt (63). Nearby are the remains of Stump Cross (NZ 794134), (Woodwarks No 9) which is possibly the Roger Cross of Danby Boundary 1660. The site of the Danby Beacon (975ft) is another wonderful viewpoint described by Atkinson in 'Forty Years' (64). The old track makes for the large group of coal pits called Castleton Pits, joining with those at Clitherbeck, further west.

An enclosure road called Poverty Hill Lane descends Oakley Side steeply, from NZ 727085. It meets the road to Duck Bridge across the Esk, built 1390 (see p59). From there paved trods follow the roads up to Danby castle and to Ainthorpe by Kadelands. Most of the flags remain along both routes south of Duck Bridge though some have gone recently from the Claymire Gate near the Methodist Chapel. It was here that Canon Atkinson relates that the witch "Au'd Nanny" ran in her clogs frightening a lad who tried to stop her (65). "Within a mile of Danby Vicarage, is a place where the old flagged causeway between all or most of Cleveland used to run".

Another paved trod leads from Castleton southwards along the foot of the Howe (NZ 693077) by the side of the road Wandles Lane, now surfaced. Wandels were early arable fields divided between the peasants in Doles or strips marked by Wands. The road continues to Tofts Lane and by St Hilda's Church. It goes on through Church Wood and Lumley Green Wood and may have continued by Gate Way to Botton.

EGTON BRIDGE - EGTON - WESTONBY

A flagged path leads from Lelum Hall (NZ 804054) at 200ft above the river up to Hill Wood where it climbs steeply on the side of a small stream on a curving terrace. Flags are about the usual width, 2ft by 18ins, 4- 6ins thick and close set. Tooling is visible, there is not a lot of wear, and they are raised in parts. It leads up to Causeway Howes: a field name on an Egton Estate Map of 1636, which may be a date for its origin. It runs due north to join Egton Lane at the junction of the path to the old St. Hilda's Church, which was dismantled in 1871 and replaced by the present mortuary chapel. The foundations of the old church are on the west, probably 12th century in date. The paved trod leads by the church site and descends the steep Church Cliff on the west. There is a bank 8ft wide and 3ft high on the edge of this cliff. It runs for 64ft with a hollow-way on the north-east side. In the field to the east eroded potsherds of calcite-gritted ware are found on the surface and the sexton has dug up two Roman coins and a rim of late 4th century cook-pot ware. It is an excellent site for a signal station or beacon.

The track is lost in places, but paving was uncovered in a short trench near Cliff Hill Bridge (NZ 797067). The bridge is built of large slabs on a central pillar, with paving stones 2-3ft wide by 18-20ins, showing wear in the centre.

On the north-west side of the bridge the causeway was replaced by a road 10ft 6ins wide, probably made from former paving. It seems to lead to Westonby House Farm (NZ 793072), site of a lost village (66). Howe House nearby was re-built by the Fosters of Egton in 1884. The howe is still traceable on a natural hill east of the farmhouse. There was a coal mine at the head of Church Dale but it was only of poor quality.

A paved footpath from the cemetery follows Egton Lane into the village. It joins that running down to Egton Bridge on the side of the present road past the 19th century church which has been restored recently.

From Egton Village a road, which has now lost its flags, runs north-east near the former racecourse, which was still unenclosed in 1853. The base and shaft of a cross at NZ 811068 were shown on the 1853 OS map. Old tracks cross to the north-west, probably joining the Guisborough-Whitby road. To the east is a group of three or four tumuli. This area has been enclosed since 1853.

On Egton Low Moor another old track is shown, coming up from Grosmont Priory via Cotebank Farm. Here a stone inscribed CXL was thought to be a Roman milestone, but is more likely Cote Bank and Lamplands - the adjoining farm. It passes tumuli and goes under the plantation to join the main Guisborough-Whitby road at Lady Cross Gate on the line of Cucket Nook Park Dike (NZ 800088, ref 67). Lady Cross (NZ 817085) has gone; broken by roadmen in 1939. It had on it GUIS..... ROAD 1771 and WHITBY RO (and faintly AD) on the east side.

The track from Egton to Aislaby divided at NZ 829073, near Water Gate Ford and a plantation and several old quarries - the largest, 'Cooper's Quarry' just above Topstone Folly (p24). One branch follows the present road to Aislaby the other passes through a group of cairns (possibly just old field clearance). It is visible as a deep hollow-way south of the three tumuli at Andrew Howe (NZ 837083). It passes by East Bank Farm (NZ 838084, now Moorcock) and over Kempstone Rigg. Here at NZ 841087, stands a plain shaft with dates of boundary ridings of the eighteenth century, 1774 and later. Young (68) says it replaced a carved shaft of Saxon type, Swarth Howe Cross. At NZ 843086 the track divides into twin hollow-ways merging into the A171 at the top of Skelder, about three and a half miles west of Whitby.

At Swarth Howe the A171 is crossed at its highest point in this area, at 854ft. The track passes the Grey Stone, (mentioned in 1206) and enters the large Skelder Plantation. Here it is confined between two turf banks, 54ft apart, no doubt the result of enclosure before 1850. In March 1966, a section of this road was excavated (69) (Fig 3). The raised central portion was over 25ft wide - cambered ridge of yellow shale only lightly metalled with a single layer of stones or cobbles, about 12ft wide, without kerbs. On the south-east was a shallow ditch or hollow-way 8-9ft wide and 18ins deep. There were no finds of any period. The late R.J.M. Rastall of Grosmont and others thought this was part of the Roman Road, leading to Dunum Sinus (Dunsley). However, although there is a medieval chapel site at Dunsley (NZ 857112) and medieval sherds have been found (70) nothing Roman has been discovered. The line follows through Skelder plantation and continues as a deep hollow-way for 300 yards then turns north-east to meet the road to Dunsley and Raven Hill (NZ 865122) where it descends to the sea.

A former brewery at East Row, just to the west was said to be on the site of a temple of Thor! The name Thorbisa appears in the 12th century when William de Percy, in a charter, mentions "the fountain or spring where Thuf lies". Young says Disa was the wife of Thor - actually the Disar were attendant deities or Fates and Thor's wife was Sif (71).

On the south side of Dunsley smithy there was a cambered road or path turning down to Raithwaite. It was only about 10ft in width. Other flagged paths go north-west of Newholm to Dunsley and Raithwaite from Mires Lane and Back Lane,

Newholm.

EGTON - AISLABY - BRIGGSWATH - WHITBY

Egton was important in medieval and post-medieval times. It had a thriving fair and market, held until the late 19th century. Egton Town Hall, which was also used as a market hall, pinfold and lock-up, was only dismantled in 1880 (72). It had a racecourse on the former moor fields marked on the 1850 OS map and so presumably still in use, opposite the site of the cross mentioned on p22. Just north of this is a guide post marking an old winding lane leading to Aislaby. This passes by Watergate and Horsemire Head to another Watergate north-east of the CXL stone above Cote Bank (see p23); further east at Coopers Farm a track veers north-east towards Topstone Folly. On the slope above the farm after ploughing in 1954, were found a few pieces of Roman pottery, round and saddle querns, six box-like structures of thin stone slabs, over fifty flints, burnt stones and quartz pebbles, possibly heavily burnt-pot boilers. This area was investigated in connection with Wade's Causeway (73, see p29).

Further east are several old quarries, part of the Aislaby series. A section of the track leading up to them at NZ 836078 was excavated (Fig 4). It was laid on a cambered ridge 8ft wide, the steeper slope on the south side with a gutter on the north-west. The paving stones were 2ft 6ins by 6ins thick, worn hollow on top, set on the south-east side of the ridge, with a gutter on the north-west. Between the slabs and gutter was 4ft of thin cobbling. This track seemed to end at a quarry 250 yards further east, though a branch led up to Cooper's Quarry and onto Kempstone Rigg. A deep hollow-way curved downhill to join the Aislaby Road below Howcam Plantation. The latter road is cambered here; this led Dr. Elgee to think it might be part of Wades Causeway.

Two hundred yards south of this section on the side of Old Park Lane, leading to Newbiggin Hall (NZ 836073) some of the Whitby Naturalists Club members found stones, querns and native Roman pottery in 1964-5 (74). Further examination proved it to be the floor of a round hut, not part of the Roman road as was thought at first. The pottery was mainly 4th century AD but the most interesting finds were of worked and unworked jet including three cores of 'chuck' discarded from lathe working and part of a slender jet bracelet. This is the earliest recorded jet workshop in the Whitby district. 300 yards south runs part of the well-preserved pannier-way from Grosmont to Sleights (p25).

The Aislaby road keeps on the 4-500ft contour through the village with fine views of lower Eskdale and Whitby. From the east end of the village some stretches of a paved footpath run alongside the modern Aislaby Lane to join the A171 at Hawthorndale.

At NZ 864083 the famous Featherbed Lane winds sharply downhill for 400ft to Briggswath. It is paved all the way apart from where the modern road A169 crosses it at Sleights. According to Sewell it was reputed to be "the narrowest high-road in England" (75) - being licensed as such during the Stuart period. He says it formed part of the King's High Road between Whitby and Kirkbymoorside, although I very much doubt whether travellers to Kirkbymoorside would have followed the route given by Sewell.

The toll bar at its foot was on the 'new' turnpike of 1760. Sleights had one of the first stone bridges over the Esk built about AD 1200, doubtless following a wooden bridge earlier - there was a Roman settlement close by (76). A later stone bridge was swept away by the great flood of July 23rd, 1930. The modern bridge spans a greater height, but the road on the Carrs still has water over it in flood times. Sewell records the building of a bridge here in 1720 (77).

At the sharp bend on Ruswarp Bank on the east side the remains of a medieval pottery kiln was found in 1980 behind houses nos. 11-12 on the Bank. The pottery was well-fired and possibly 12th-13th century AD. Tiles were also manufactured here. Perhaps most of the products were shipped from Whitby, but a sherd from Stokesley of this ware must have been carried by pack or pannier (78). Sewell says: "The inhabitants of Ruswarp are indicted for not repairing the highway between the market towns of Whitby and Kirby" (79). He thought the Roman Road connected with Kirkbymoorside but this is an unfounded guess. No one has traced it north of the Esk, and Young's statement that it was crossed by the Guisborough Road at the third milestone out of Whitby has never been proved (80).

GROSMONT - SLEIGHTS (MONKS TROD)

Immediately west of Grosmont Priory at NZ 828059 the late R.J.M. Rastall with the Wilkinsons of Sleights excavated a piece of road that had stones laid on the north side like a kerb. R.W. Crosland and I re-dug this in November 1945 and sections were drawn (81). It consisted of a cambered ridge of gravel and yellow shale 12ins high and 17-18ft wide. On this a layer of clay 3-4ins thick and a metalling of river-stones. The regular kerb on the north side had stones averaging 14 by 10 by 8ins. No definite kerb could be found on the south side. As Young said "a considerable part of the Roman Road was dug west of the Priory about 1800" (80). We thought this was a section, but as J.G. Rutter pointed out, it is significant that the piece we found lies on the same line as the flagged path to Briggswath, near Sleights and could be the same age and purpose. It would be handy for the Priory with its connections with Whitby and the harbour for fish, etc.

The paved trod went up into Dorsley Bank Wood where it is visible near Fotherleys Farm between modern concrete tracks. It is in good condition the whole way from Fotherleys Farm to Woodlands, over two miles. The path is known as the Monks Trod locally. From Fotherleys to NZ 835066 it turns up the wood with a holloway to the north-west. Flags are displaced at intervals and it is muddy at times. It passes the north end of the wood and crosses the field with a sharp bend to the north. It turns by some oak trees at the junction of Old Park Lane where another line of paving stones comes from the north-west from Haystones.

The main trod passes close to Newbiggin Hall and forms the muddy farm road. The Salvins had Newbiggin Hall in the 14th century. It has been rebuilt in the last century though there are still traces of a moat. The trod is eroded on the north side of Hecks Wood. It crosses the pasture to Back Wood where it is lost in scrub and undergrowth. Above Newbiggin Lodge it turns south-east and crosses a ravine close to a footbridge. It is visible in places in fields to Thistle Grove; with flags which are worn but in line. It joins the modern road at Woodlands and there is a track to Groves Hall and Briggswath. It is followed on most of its line by a public footpath. An alternative line could have gone from the river up Brook Park (Briggswath) and followed the footpath by Lumbert (now Lambert) Hill avoiding Turnerdale Slack to join the Whitby road at the Ashes above Ruswarp Bank (82).

SLEIGHTS - IBURNDALE - SNEATON
(SNEATON CAUSEWAY OR MONKS WALK)

South of the Esk the village street through Sleights climbs gradually then steeply to the Blue Bank. Halfway up at St. John's Church, Dale Lane on the east has a paved path to Iburndale, where a branch turns south to the water-mill. A portion of paving still exists at the mill. It may have continued up the dale by the weir with a branch up Dale Lane and crossed by the Blue Bank road. It may have turned north at Eskdale Gate towards the Eskdale Chapel, (NZ 860073). This is the supposed site of a hermitage of 1159, but from the remains it was at least in existence in the 14th century. It has recently been consolidated. It is not far from the Esk and a wooden bridge here would have given access to the paved way from Grosmont. Stone flags are still visible under soil and vegetation running down most of the west side of the concrete farm road from Eskdale Gate to the Chapel.

The Dale Lane continues from Iburndale twisting round to Ugglebarnby, a Norse place-name meaning 'Owl-Beard'. It had an ancient Norman Church, replaced in 1872 by the structure built by local gentry and villagers. The village has a rare relic, a Moot Stone where the forerunner of our parish meetings was held. It was stipulated that it must always be kept uncovered and not used for 'sand braying' (83). From Pasture Fields east of the church the paved way can be followed via Force Hall and well to Plainsides Farm and on to a footbridge south of Sneaton Hall. At Sneaton it ran on the north side of the road to a junction at the eastern end of the village. A short stretch remains. There is a gap, then it is visible in the pasture field at Sneaton Beacon (NZ 898077).

The north trod goes down Shawn Rigg (Helm Rigg), called Sneaton Causeway or Monk's Walk (84). This section NZ 898090, is one of the best remaining. It goes down a narrow overgrown lane to the beck and foot- bridge, then turns over Shawn Riggs descending abruptly to Cock Mill Wood by a flight of stone steps, some single, some double, with pitched stones on edge to hold them firm. A modern footbridge replaces the old stone culvert here over two becks - Mill Beck and Stainsacre Beck. In Larpool Wood the trod turns sharply north-west at a steep 1 in 3 angle above the former Larpool Hall. Near Larpool Hall trods have been replaced by modern paving and further traces are obliterated. Sewell (85) thought it went on the east bank of the Esk to Spitalbridge. It could have gone by Crowdy Hall to the Mount, and on the south bank to Whitby Bridge, or across the Esk by the Boghall Ford, which could be crossed at low water. (Plate 8)

The Misses Horseman and Haigh also describe a paved trod running north-south from near the lane to Rigg Mill following the top of Long Rigg to Cock Mill (NZ 900089), called 'Kocche' Mill, in the 11th century. It has now gone, along with the fine wooden wheel of Rigg Mill further down the beck. Stones of the Long Rigg trod were 24 by 21ins and 7ins thick.

The line south from Sneaton Beacon (NZ 898077) is visible for a few yards, but then is lost. It followed the line of the present footpath to Sneaton Thorpe Lane. There is no trace of the line due south but more stones are visible in the village of Sneaton Thorpe at NZ 906063. Mr. Sleightholme told Misses Horseman and Haigh (in 1964) that paving flags were visible in the grass verge in a corner near Mortar Pit Farm (NZ 906068) but they were removed by county highways men. At Sneaton Thorpe, a tiny hamlet with a good example of a long-house, the trod crosses a beck by a stone slab 9ft long 2ft wide, only 3-4ins thick and 3ft above the summer level of the stream. The trod turns east over a smaller brigstone about 4 by 2ft 4-5ins thick, where ten stone slabs form steps. It then turns towards Long Rigg (NZ 913062, now called Rigg Farm) and Stainsacre Lane. From Soulgrave Slack it joins the modern road near Long Rigg. Turning south towards the present lane, Catwick Farm lies to the south-west; there are a few stones here.

AROUND WHITBY

PICKERING - WHITBY

The Roman Road, Wade's Causeway (p29), only climbs to 826 ft when crossing the moors -lower than most of the later roads which all rise to 1000ft or over, with consequent difficulty in winter snow.

The medieval routes between Pickering and Whitby could be varied. The main one probably went up by Newbridge quarry (SE 802858) and today winds gently up the limestone slack by Haugh Howl (a narrow ravine) to Haugh Rigg where quarries line its sides and several small squarish enclosures produce Roman and native pottery (86). One of them on the hillside south of Cooks Grange is called Old Roman Camp on the Keldy Estate map of 1873. The road went to the junction with the roads from Cropton and Newton on Rawcliffe at Stape Bank Top. It passes Rawcliffe Howe, supposed burial place of an early king of Pickering, Peredurus, said by local tradition to be laid here (87), but the tumulus was more likely erected 2,000 years earlier. Deep hollow-ways wind down the west side of Stape Bank. The present road is in one of them. Stape is a straggling village, with turf walls around its fields, some now replaced with wire fences. The Roman Wade's Causeway came in from the south between the Chapel and the Band Room (now a house). Both roads follow the same line over the ford at the north end of the village by the former Hare and Hounds Inn. They pass Old Wife's Well, a spring on the east side of the present road now on the edge of the forest. Here the Romans and the drovers or travellers to Whitby could have a drink. It supplied Stape with drinking water until the late 19th century. The stone on top had inscribed on it 'NATTIE FONTEN'. It would be most unusual for the word Fonten to be used for a spring in North Yorkshire: Keld is the local word. The rather roughly inscribed word may be a corruption of 'Fons Natalis' the name of a Celtic Water Nymph. It is now surrounded by conifers and unless the path is kept open will be lost in the jungle.

At NE 796944 Mauley Cross marks the highest point, 825ft. It was a boundary of the lands of the De Mauley family of Mulgrave Castle north-west of Whitby. Malo Cross north-east of Saltergate has the same origin (p32). The medieval road slanted off east-north-east towards Brown Howe. There is now a reservoir on top of the howe where part of a jet bangle was found, but no excavation took place. Brown Howe Cross stood north of the howe. Its predecessor was taken by Dr. Kirk for his collection, which formed the basis for the Castle Museum in York, where the cross is now thought to be. Before it was ploughed up and planted with conifers the road was raised and cambered 16ft wide on Gale Hill and called Blawath Road from the beck of that name it crosses further north. This section crosses by two deep holloways and seems to curve towards Howl Moor and Hunt House, mentioned in the 14th century Thomas de Honthous 1301 (88).

The line used for the Post Road to Whitby (p28) most likely ran south of Brown Howe (NZ 808951) to Wardle Rigg and Green where small farmhouses remain. Wardle Rigg, one of the few Celtic place names in north-east Yorkshire, means the 'Rigg above the dale of the Welshmen', Wal or Weal being the ancient term for Britons. (Wheeldale is from the same source.) The enclosures at Wardle Rigg may be Celtic fields.

At Wardle Green the old track emerges from the forest through the heather to Simon Howe, 850ft. Its name may mean Simon's burial mound according to place-name experts.

The road passes on the west side where pannier paving was noted after a disastrous fire in 1947. The howe was mutilated by pot-hunting squires in the 19th century, and lately by too many walkers, as the Lyke Wake Walk passes over it. There was a row of five upright stones pointing to a very eroded mound on the north-east end of the ridge (850ft). Two tracks go north-west and north-east, one towards the Two Howes and Goathland, passing above 'The Killing Pits' (SE 821999), thought to be old pitfalls for game, but most likely bell-pits for iron ore which was smelted at New Wath in the valley below. The main track went near Thornhill Farm down into Goathland to Abbot's House. Abbots Bridge is on the site of the old pack-horse bridge that has long gone, with the inn that replaced Abbot's House. This was a place of refreshment for the old travellers. When the monks held the Abbot's House they provided food and shelter for the travellers, but this ceased at the Dissolution. When the house was sold each new owner was required to blow a horn on Sil Howe, and this was observed until 80 years ago. The little Wayside Inn was built to serve the wayfarers, but when the railway was laid in 1863 the license was transferred to the Station Hotel.

The poor state of the road in the 18th century and measures attempted to improve it are described on p34.

Abbot's House lane led onto the moor and joined the line of the present road to Sil Howe (NZ 852028), a tumulus levelled some time ago for road improvements. Sewell says there were three roads leading to Sil Howe (89) and he calls the main one, described above, as the Pike Hill road - a name derived from the turnpike. The second led from Morton Close (NZ 828036 formerly Malton Close, a house once held by the Malton Priory) and Beckhole. (The third is the modern road). The main track continued over Goathland Moor to Blue Bank above Sleights. It then followed the north bank of the Esk to Ruswarp and Whitby.

Sewell also says "I am told by two authorities there exist lengths of stones in line crossing the moor between Foster Howes (NZ 875009) and Abbot's Farm at Goathland, which probably represent a branch of the Pannierman's Track to the ancient hermitage" (84). He goes on to say that it was spoken of as "the smugglers road". The stones he mentions still exist in parts although buried by the peat. On the 1853 OS map this line is called Old Post Road, marked by dotted lines, but they do not always correspond with the existing flag-stones. The Old Post Road was used by the Malton-Whitby postman who was appointed in 1662 (90).

About 120 yards south of Widow Howe (NZ 859000) the first trace of flags appear and can still be followed along Widow Howe Rigg to a point some 700 yards south-west of the Foster Howes (91). A boggy holloway runs on the north side of the stones. It soon converges into the causeway, the flags being tilted over into the bog. They are set into a bank over three yards wide and one yard high in places; the hollows continue on both sides, further up the slope 4-6 feet wide. Stones of the trod were 3ft by 18ins and vary in thickness. There is no sign of wear on the exposed slabs, though they are mostly covered with ling. The trod curves south-west of the larger, southern most Foster Howe (NZ 875009). There is no raised ridge of the trod nor signs of the hollow-way along the last 300 yards to the howe. It is lost east of the howes but found turning north-east towards the Whinstone Ridge, a volcanic rift; here at NZ 876018 the flags cross another older track called High Street coming from Sil Howe and Robbed Howe in a south-easterly direction. The trod is lost near York (or John or Jack) Cross, 300 yards to the south-east.

York Cross (92) does not appear to have any recognisable track near it. Sewell (93) says, "it has only the mound and stone base left". Certainly the plain shaft over 3ft high, is not weathered, unlike the base. Sewell says York Cross and Pannierman's Howe (one of the Foster Howes?) are names of recent origin. Here the trod turns down towards Falling Foss where a few stones remain, but much has been destroyed by the Forestry Commission's plantations.

It ascends to Red Gate (NZ 892045), where it joins the modern B1416 down to Ruswarp. There was no metalled road in 1850, just a footpath running due north on the line of Belt Plantation. A possible line is by Ugglebarnby Moor to the Buskey Buskey Gill Quarry and Dean Hall where paving continues to South House and

Ugglebarnby (p26). The direct line which went from the road at NZ 891056 north-north-east to near Sneaton Post Office, (and continues as the Monk's Walk) was ploughed out for half a mile by 1910, though a footpath followed it to Knaggy House (NZ 899060) and further east to Sneatonthorpe; thence to Whitby by the routes mentioned on p26.

Even in the mid 18th century travellers were advised to hire a local guide to cross the moors to Malton and York. As traffic increased in the early 18th century turnpike trusts were empowered to collect tolls for the upkeep of these roads. The turnpike road from Malton to Whitby is thought to have been constructed under the terms of an Act of 1764, although Sewell uses the Ogilby map to suggest 1760 (94). It follows the course of modern roads but goes by Thornton Dale, joining the modern A169 at The Fox and Rabbit north of Pickering.

On the 1854 OS map a road called Scampston Way is shown coming from Newton Dale near Pifflehead to cross by the A169 at the elbow of Saltergate Bank. On the opposite (east) side of the bank behind the present car park, is another old track called Old Wife's Way. The same name is given to the Roman road over Wheeldale Moor 'The Old Wife's Trod'. The road to Pickering goes by Kingthorpe and has a cross-ridge dike on either side, possibly used as a check point for early travellers. In the Coucher Book there is a tale of a game warden extracting a due from people crossing here (14).

A little house on the east side of the present road near Saltergate bridge is still called Barr Farm and it indicates a toll collection point or bar. The turnpike followed the line of the present road by Ellerbeck and Brocka Beck. It is shown on Jeffery's map of 1775 following the line still used here.

The Goathland road joins it at Sil Howe where it turns more north-east to the top of Blue Bank. This was rather notorious in the early days of motoring but much improved today. The view of the coast is fine with Whitby Abbey in the centre.

Passing through Sleights it crosses the Esk by a modern bridge replacing the one washed away in 1930, which avoided the old road on the river bank which was liable to flooding. It ascends to join the Guisborough road near Cross Butts. Only the base of the former medieval cross remains. It descends into Whitby by Airy Hill where the road to Scarborough crosses the Esk by a new high level bridge, opened in 1978.

Coaches began to make regular journeys to York and in 1788 when there was a twice weekly service. This was succeeded in 1795 by a mail coach three times a week. Scarborough had a service to Whitby meeting another at Flask Inn (95).

At first the roads were paved with any local stone mainly limestone south of Saltergate and whinstone above. Parts were tarred in the early 1920s when some motor traffic began but the road as a whole was not tarred until the 1930s when traffic increased in volume.

WADES CAUSEWAY
(AMOTHERBY - CAWTHORN - LEASE RIGG).

Reference has already been made to Wade's Causeway, the only certain Roman Road in North East Yorkshire. It is the subject of the report under the same name published by the author and J.G. Rutter in 1964 (59). In this report we took Wades Causeway from its crossing of the Malton Street at Amotherby northwards to Lease Rigg, Grosmont, where it appears to be heading towards the coast just north of Whitby, although its terminus has not yet been found. According to Herman Ramm (96) it connected York with this coastal area though there is no evidence that it served the late 4th century signal stations. Rutter insisted it was aligned on the Wade stone near East Barnby, but no Roman site has been found here.

The stretch south of Amotherby was examined before our study began. It is now followed by a deep hollow-way beside a line of several pre-Roman tumuli to the line of Braygate Street running west from Malton. It may have curved here to connect with a small portion of kerbed and cambered road at Brandrith Farm, south of Bulmer which was ploughed out in 1955. It was 30ft wide with side ditches which produced Roman pottery and tiles. P. Corder, the excavator thought there was a building nearby.

It crossed the Vale of Pickering through Great Barugh and Wrelton and climbed towards Cawthorn. There is a field at Cawthorn called Little Street Close, and the Saxon word street often marks the existence of a Roman road. Over Wheeldale it was called the Ald Gate in the 14th century, and the ford at the bottom of Wheeldale Gill was 'Standwath' or stone-ford. The Wheeldale section was uncovered 1912-20 and is still uncovered and visited by many. On the slope south of this ford the road has a central rib of large boulders. It does not show wear and possibly had a thick layer of smaller stones on top. The lane from the ford to Hazel Head is on the old line but the paving has sunk here. See p33 for more details and its route near Goathland. (Plate 10)

North of the Esk few traces are left. It was thought to pass near Grosmont Priory, but here it is confused with the later flagged trod (p25). Near Lythe is a High Street although there is no known Roman association.

The conclusion on Wade's Causeway was that it could be an early military road of AD 80-120 when it fell into disuse and there is little evidence that it was re-used in the late 4th century. What is left now even on Wheeldale Moor is merely the foundation.

THE OLD SALT ROAD or ROBIN HOOD'S BAY ROAD (SALTERGATE - ROBIN HOOD'S BAY)

This road has been mentioned many times in guide-books and popular accounts. It is shown on the 1853 OS map and on the Knox map 1855; both show roughly the same course for the road.

It starts near The Saltergate Inn, (SE 852943) 12 miles south of Whitby. This inn is reputed to take its name from traffic in salt from the coastal salt pans (97). The salt was carried in rectangular blocks by the panniermen and kept by users in stone troughs with a small aperture, or door. These salt boxes were a regular feature of the hearth place in old moorland farmhouses and there are examples in the Ryedale Folk Museum.

The Salt (or Fish Road as it was also often called) was not paved, as far as the remains show today. It was a series of hollow tracks, keeping on dry ground where possible, and some sections show several parallel routes.

On the maps of 1853 and 1855 it is shown to branch from the 1760 turnpike at a wooden guide post (now gone) 1 miles north of the inn. From this junction it went north-east to a stone called Trough Stone at NZ 858970 possibly the base of a vanished cross though there is no mention of a cross in Woodwark's booklet. The moor is called Tom Cross Rigg. The route of the road turns eastwards over Snod Hill (850ft) now covered by the Fylingdales Early Warning Station, and fenced off, although the Lyke Wake track passes around the perimeter fence. After running due east for about a mile the Salt Road turns to cross Ellerbeck at Coach Wath and curves round by Worm Syke (Hagworm Syke?) on to steadily rising ground accompanied by hollow-ways on the north side. It is now joining the main ridgeway followed by the Pannierman's Road (p31) turning north and climbing to 950ft at its highest point.

Here stands Lilla Cross on Lilla Howe (NZ 889987). This has always been presumed to be the Burial Mound of Lilla, the Saxon thane who saved the life of King Edwin from assassination in AD 628. Supposed Saxon ornaments were found in the howe but they are now dated to the Viking age, 200 years later than Lilla's time

(98). This high point is a notable junction. Tracks and hollow-ways criss-cross and the Lyke Wake Walkers pass that way towards Ellerbeck and Goathland. (Plate 12)

The Salt Road goes north-east alongside Green Swang to Cock Lake Side and over the boggy Biller Howe Dale through some impressive Cross-Ridge Dikes, where there were some hundreds of small stony cairns - all bulldozed away in clearing up the army range in the 1950s. This is John or Jack Cross Rigg but all that is left of the cross is a damaged base. The Salt Road turns north-east to Thorn Key Wath (NZ 914032) where a confusing number of tracks cross in all directions. By Thorn Key Howes is a ring cairn, a bank of earth and stones around Bronze Age burials. There are standing stones of the same period, to the east above Ramsdale. The main road A171 is crossed at Latter Gate Hill (tumuli) and the modern road leads down to Robin Hood's Bay.

The Salt Road was used by carts, sleds and other vehicles in the past. Sewell says, "About 1888 the late John Rowland, Esq., of Goathland, drove and had carried where necessary, a light four-wheeled basket carriage from the neighbourhood of John Cross Howe along the old Robin Hood's Bay Road via Lilla Cross to Goathland. He told the writer that this was the last time the road was used. Some fourteen years later, when walking over this track it was found to consist of lengths of road, some of which were separated by gullies 30ft across" (99). In 1937 Harry Flynn of Beverley and I wheeled and in places rode bicycles, over the same route, taking three hours from Saltergate to cross over to Robin Hood's Bay. (Plate 11a)

THE PANNIERMAN'S ROAD OR CAUSEWAY (SIL HOWE - HACKNESS)

Another Pannierman's Road, unpaved this time, runs from Sil Howe to Hackness. This road branches off the Sleights road at Sil Howe (NZ 852028) and goes east along the Whinstone Ridge by an unnamed tumulus at 900ft just south of the modern A169. It passes Robbed Howe, with a boundary stone of Whitby Strand. Then it runs east of the boundary on York Cross (also known as John or Jack Cross) Rigg (p28) where it was crossed by the old Whitby Road 400 yards south-west of York Cross. It follows Foster Howe Rigg southwards to a point east of Ann's Cross (100) (NZ 878000). Further south-south-east on Stony Leas (975ft), stands Louven Howe, a tumulus. Sewell calls it Louvain Cross (101) saying, - "it was possibly erected by Agnes, Sister of Alan de Percy, who married Joceline of Louvain, and he took his wife's name". He says it has a Maltese Cross carved on the central stone and that a well had been sunk into the mound of the howe, its mouth being some 6ft above the moor level. The stone now appears to have fallen but where did the water come from as the howe is on top of the ridge? There are hints of a wolf-pit as on Danby Fryup Rigg and elsewhere. South of Louven Howe (980ft) the Robin Hood's Bay road branches north-east at a modern guide-post. A parallel track goes north of Burn Howe Duck Pond (SE 896991).

The Pannierman's Road runs south-east to another Brown Hill at SE 920979 (679ft). It then follows the ridge of Lownorth Moor to Harwood Dale, crossing the beck at Park Hill near Castlebeck and Chapel Farm, which takes its name from the ruined St. Margaret's Church, one of the three Hackness churches (96). Further south the present road starts to climb Reasty Hill about 'Pits' wood where ironstone was obtained by the bell pit method. Smelting took place at Cinder Hills (SE 971947) where there was a huge heap of slag, examined by Peter Farmer of the Scarborough & District Society in 1968. The bloomery was not found but he thought the site was 13th-16th century, though there was a hint of earlier working.

Reasty Hill top is a notable viewpoint for Harwood Dale, though the east is screened by plantations. To the south over Silpho Moor and Swinesgill a pleasant footpath goes down to Whisperdales and Lowdales, on to Hackness.

An alternative route, also called the Pannierman's Road runs south of Lilla Cross, curving to avoid the bogs near Derwent Head, and passing west of High and Low Woof (wolf) Howes (SE 892962). It goes south over Broad and Little Grain Head to Thornhill Head. Most of the way it is now engulfed in dense plantations of the Forestry Commission on Wykeham High Moor. The present footpath runs parallel but west of the old track and goes to Birch Hall (SE 926925) and Hackness. The old road passes Langdale End to Hackness which was a cell of Whitby Abbey, having its origin in Saxon times, and is recorded in Domesday as having three churches (102). Parts of its famous Saxon Cross remains in the present church of St. Peter's. St. John's Church may be under the lake at Hackness Hall.

There was another branch from this road south-west from Lilla Cross towards Worm Sike Rigg and skirting May Moss (a dangerous bog) towards Malo Cross at the foot of Whinny Nab (SE 867949). Woodwark says "the base and the shaft have disappeared, only a fragment of the head remains" (103). The present cross shows repairs; the head looks recent, it is rounded on top and on the ends of the arms. It is inscribed R(R)E - Sir Richard Egerton 1619, and was re-erected in 1924. Egerton was accused of 'trespass and encroachment about Blackhow, in the heart of the forest - he set up on Whenny Nab one new bounderstone with a cross and of raising stones where there were none before' (104). (Plate 9)

HIGH GATE (WHITBY - HAWSKER - ROBIN HOOD'S BAY - STAINTONDALE)

The route south from Whitby starts with the steep Church Lane, known locally as the Donkey Path which rises from Church Street to St Mary's Church parallel to the famous 199 steps.

Almost two and a half miles of flagged pathway were visible a few years ago down the coast south of Whitby. First traces were on the west side of the modern road just outside the East Wall of the Abbey although the run as far as Green Lane has been replaced by concrete slabs (105). Canon J.C. Atkinson writing in 1890 describes them. "There are old flags of the Pannierman's causey, side by side with the modern macadamized road, and these flags, no long time since still retain their position, between the upper end of Green Lane, and continued towards the Abbey House". Atkinson continues to mention the High 'Street' as a landmark in an extract from an Indenture between the Abbot of Whitby and William Page and others dated 1351: "granted to William Page and others - pasture for all manner of live stock save only pigs and goats, in the Carrs, with right of way thither by the Highway through Ruswarp, at all seasons of the year from Spoutcliff and in Ellerdale Tickets, as far as the head of Ellerdale, and in Crosskeld-syke as far as the High Street which stretches from Whitby and all the way to Hawsker" (106). No flag-stones could be found in Green Lane going south from High Gate from NZ905110 by Misses Horsman and Haigh in 1963-4 (105).

The raised bank containing the flags can be seen on the west side of the present road for about a mile between Green Lane and Highgate Howe, where it takes a sharp bend. The flags are next found on the east side of the front of Whitby Laithes, the farm of monastic origin at NZ 925095. This is a moated grange with a long range of buildings. Laith is an old name for barn. Mr. McNeill, the farmer, said there was a paved way to the oldest part of the farm at its north end. The stones are 2ft wide by 4ins thick and vary from 20-30ins in length. Near Red Barn, (NZ 923086) they are under clay for some 220 yards; where visible 2ft 9ins long by 2ft wide and 3ft long by 6ins thick.

From Red Barn to Hawsker School the stones are under soil or grass and some modern paving. Further towards Hawsker stones were observed being re-laid in 1964, 23-25ins long by 26ins wide, 4ins thick of yellow-brown sandstone with traces of iron, slightly hollowed in the centre (105).

From High Hawsker eastwards on the Robin Hood's Bay road to the corner at NZ

932075 flags were visible in 1963-64, but were removed with road works in 1972. They can be seen at intervals on the west side of the modern road to Robin Hood's Bay near East Close Spring. There was no trace of any along Bottom's Lane (eastwards towards Hawsker Bottoms), apart from a few under the old hedge (105).

On the coast north of Hawsker Bottoms is Gnipe Howe (SE 935085) and coal used to be mined on the face of the cliff. The only path down it was used by pack animals from the mine and was known locally as 'Jackass Trod' (107).

No paving was found in Low Hawsker where the shaft of a Saxon cross still stands (108).

Paved footpaths probably continued from Hawsker to Robin Hood's Bay, though several have gone with later alterations to modern roads.

From Fyling Park Gate (NE 937046) Sledgate runs north-east towards Fylingthorpe and passes through the village to join Ling Lane and turns south-east to 'Bay'. There is later paving on this line.

Further south of Middle Wood paving continues to a footbridge to South House (NZ 951038) where the path has been destroyed and blocked. The line is picked up again running south-east to Stoupe Beck Wood (NZ 954033) where it may have gone to the beach or crossed to Stoupe Brow Bank. A branch from the above trod diverges at NZ 948040, turning south-west to cross Mill Beck and turning west at the site of Owlet Hall (NZ 945035) towards Fylinghall but the line has been disturbed by the railway (now disused).

South of Fyling Old Hall there are stones left in a line south from Howdale Wood to Thorny Brow (NZ 947016) on Howdale Moor edge. At 450ft it is now uninhabited, but is an interesting old farmhouse of three periods with upper-crucks in the west bay. Fyling Park was an important deer park of the Abbot of Whitby. It is shown on the OS maps. The Park Pale is a substantial stone wall, of roughly squared stones, with others laid in the form of a cross at intervals of approximately 50ft, several of which survive (109).

Stoupe Brow was on a very ancient north-south route from Whitby by Staintondale, where at Bell Hill (NZ 985999), local legend has it that King Stephen gave the manor of Staintondale to the Knights Templars, for keeping a priest there, and helping travellers by blowing a horn and ringing a bell at night or in foggy conditions, which are very prevalent on this coast (110).

Frank Rimington of Burniston, former chairman of the Scarborough Archaeological and Historical Society, has produced a major work on Staintondale and Bell Hill (223) including details of medieval charters, granting the inhabitants of the district exemption from tax. As late as the present century some waggons had "TAX FREE" painted on their sides. He thinks there was a Roman road linking the signal stations or coastguard forts from Whitby on the line of the High gate and continuing below Stoup Brow to Ravenscar Roman Fort (now under the Ravenhall Hotel). Hinderwell mentions ruins (about 160 ft square - the base of the tower?) where the well-known inscription was found in 1774. It calls the tower 'Turrem castrum'. It was very like the numerous turrets on Hadrian's Wall. The lettering is degenerate in contrast with the well-carved examples found at York and other Roman sites. It dates from the very end of the 4th century. In the Ravenhall Hotel is a very good photograph of the stone. The road possibly continued south on the line of the present War Dike Lane to Hayburn Wyke and Scarborough.

GOATHLAND AREA

Though only tiny until the late 19th century, this village had at least two important early roads passing close by, or through it. The route of Wade's Causeway (p29) crossed Wheeldale Beck by a ford called Standworth, or in the 15th century

Stanedwayte(SE 812991, south-west of Goathland). Wade's Causeway can still be traced up the muddy lane to Hazel Head, and its ridge can be seen on what was Hazel Head Green. A section has been excavated south-west of Hollin House (111). From this point it takes a winding course owing to the hilly terrain, passing close to Julian Park, long thought to be of Roman origin, but almost certainly a mansion or hunting lodge of the De Mauleys of Mulgrave. It is now a farmhouse, the ancient building having been demolished about 1860. It is likely there was a turf maze here. The name St. Julian's is a clue as Julian's Bower is the name of the Horncastle turf maze in Lincolnshire (112). The Roman road went on to Lease Rigg where a small fort has been partly excavated recently (113).

The other important medieval road was the one described on p27, from Pickering to Whitby. It was in a bad state in the 18th century. The surveyor appointed by the village still had to see that the people of Goathland came each year to do 'Statute labour' working several days and if the job was not done properly he could make an assessment for repairs. Marshall in 1790 said "farmers used marl from Newtondale; paying 1/- per wagon load to bring it three-four miles up a winding road over the top of a mountain to Goathland". Even as late as 1870 the village road was not metalled further than Wheat Hill farm, and the road from the Church to Ellerbeck was known as "New Road", the Goathland end traced by wheel tracks through the heather.

Mrs. Hollings in her book on Goathland (114) says "there were no stone causeways or hard trods in Tudor times - these came later". She gives an assessment of sixpence in the pound in 1715 for a causeway to be made between Goathland and Beckhole. Much of it still remains, though some has been lost in road widening. It went through a snicket in a field on the side of the present road progressing down the steepest part of the hill by stone steps (NZ 822/4/021/2). A wooden footbridge spanned the beck at the bottom - the ford used by cattle. The Justice of the Quarter Sessions directed some of the cash to repair Goathland Bridge on Eller Beck near Abbot's House.

The flagged trod from Beckhole went north-west to a fulling mill, long vanished, then to Blue Ber Wood noted for its oaks. There it turned west by fords and footbridge to climb to Murkside House (NZ 816031). This was formerly a typical cruck-framed long house with a hearth beam and witch post. The old house was rebuilt higher up the hillside in 1914, almost exactly on the plan of the predecessor and the hearth beam and witch post were reinstated in the new house. This was one of the few old houses with a right of way through the cross passage - the door had never to be locked (53), although the paved trod does not pass through the later (1914) house.

There are several stone trods in Goathland, recently uncovered. Other flagged paths lead to Darnholm and to the old water mill near the station.

WHITBY - LYTHE - BARNBY

The old road north-west from Whitby climbed Chubb Hill joining Flowergate and St. Hilda's Terrace, where there is now a roundabout. Upgang Lane led down onto the sands, which were followed for almost a mile to Sandsend. The road then climbed Priest's Syke to Lythe Church, very much restored in 1911, though it still has many Viking type carved stones. Near Lythe are the three Mulgrave Castles.

There is a line of pannier paving on the green west of the present Lythe Vicarage and Old Lythe Hall. These may go by a footpath south of the church, or follow the green track north very like a cambered Roman road to Overdale or possibly the other track to Deepgrove (NZ 846/8/133/40). This trod probably led to Goldsborough (NZ 836148) where a farm track with paving branches north-east from the north end of the village passing between the Roman coastal fort and Scratch Alley. This is an unusual place name, 'ORD SCRAT' was the devil in local dialect, from the sensational finds when the fort was excavated (115). They found the skeleton of a little man, much hacked about, next to it that of a larger man, and at his throat the skeleton of a large dog. No wonder the locals thought the devil had been at work. The paving is not now visible here but there is a very deep hollow-way to the north and the path continues by Kettleness Church to the cliff-top village. In the 18-19th centuries much alum was extracted here. (see Appendix E). The remains of steeping pits can be found on the end of Kettleness.

Another line of paving led south up Goldsborough Lane and was visible on the south-east side of the present road passing Barnby Howes (NZ 831139) where burials of the Beaker period were excavated in 1951 (116). Tinley Lane runs parallel to the above line from NZ 825132 going north; it has paving also. Both lead into the A174 which follows the line of Lythe High Street to Ellerby Bank Top and Newton Mulgrave, another possible Roman road.

The trod from Barnby Howes continued south through East Barnby passing Wade's Hill on the west and the Wade's Stone (NZ 831130). It has been pointed out that Wade's Causeway, the Roman road on Wheeldale Moor, is aligned on the stone near East Barnby and Goldsborough, though the Roman fort was not built until almost 350 years later and the road does not show much wear from use (117). A beehive type quern was found at East Barnby in 1970. Westgate Lane (NZ 826125) has paving and a kerb and there are hollow-ways on the east of the hill from the ford on Barnby Beck.

It has been claimed that there was a Roman road going north along the coast here, serving the coastal signal stations at Goldsborough and further north. The settlement of Street Houses at Boulby (NZ 740192) is cited as evidence of this. However, there is no real proof.

WEST BARNBY -UGTHORPE - BORROWBY

From the village opposite Barnby Lodge at NZ 818126 a causeway runs due south, crosses Scar Hill Beck by a culvert, and leads to an enclosed green lane 16ft in width. It has a raised trod in the centre, not very worn, but some large stone slabs in it, one 5-6ft long by 4ft-3ft wide; others large though less shapely. It is lost in a bog near Scar Hill, but in the green lane is visible for about a quarter of a mile. It is then lost in a deep hollow-way down to Mickleby Beck, then on to Broom House Lane which replaces the trod to Ugthorpe.

Ugthorpe Old Hall (NZ 794110) is a late 16th century house. It has very fine timber work which tallies with the inscribed date of 1586 of the Radcliffes, who lived in the Hall until after 1634. They were a Catholic family who suffered much for their faith. The Hall is only small and still a working farm.

A pannier trod can still be traced south then south-west down an overgrown lane for a mile to Traveller's Rest Farm (former inn) on the side of the A171. Here several paths lead to Woodhill Farm and Stonegate (p21). Others go to Ugthorpe Grange and Wilks Rigg.

Ugthorpe had a windmill (NZ 791115) that still retained its sails until 1936-40. Just north of the mill a hoard of silver Roman coins was ploughed up in 1792 by a boy, William Burton, who filled his pockets with them, but his master took the bulk of them and sold them to silversmiths. They were late first to early second century AD (118). The trod from the village went by the mill and it is likely others went north and west from it.

There was a trod running north from Borrowby (p20) on the north side of the present street, by a square pinfold, to some old sandstone quarries south of Keld Hill. The road continues to Dale House Mill where a decayed wooden leat bridges the beck. The late Alec Wright said that a trod apparently ran from Liverton to Loftus by Rosecroft and Red Road.

Alec Wright also recounted that a pannierway from Upleatham to Marske was destroyed about 1930.

ROSEDALE AREA

KIRKBYMOORSIDE - HUTTON LE HOLE - ROSEDALE

From Kirkbymoorside the old road to Hutton le Hole went east along Howe End then up Swinnet (Swineherd) Lane to Yoadwath (old horse ford) by a water corn mill. The area is thought to have been known as Haverbegam in a record of about 1200, and may have belonged to Keldholme Priory. In the 19th century it was worked by the Rivis family, until 1901, when a great flood washed the miller's wagon away and three horses were drowned. There is a supposed smuggler's hide-out on the opposite, north side of the ford with arched cellars for beer or whisky underneath.

The steep Yoadwath Bank climbed to join the alternative, modern road to Hutton (p11) passing on the edge of Douthwaitedale the site of a post-medieval glass furnace (119). The furnace finds are in the Ryedale Folk Museum.

The Rosedale road veers from the Hutton-Lastingham road at the top of Moor Lane and crosses a ridge to descend to Loskey Bridge, a former ford but a bridge in the mid 19th century. Here the road climbs to Spindle Thorn, where many hollow tracks converge from west of the Three Howes and Beggars' Track (p12). Some follow down Middle Rigg and most turn for Spaunton Bank or Lastingham. There must have been considerable traffic down here for no less than 30-35 parallel hollow tracks can be found at SE 718/72 910-6. Querns and grindstones came from Spaunton Moor, also much turf and peat before the later ironstone boom in 1855-1925. A track still visible runs from Spaunton Knowl to Barker Slack, Grindstone Wath and Hollins open-cast mine (SE 729945, operational 1850-70). The old road descended into Rosedale by Gill Brow later Rosedale Chimney Bank. The tall chimney was demolished in 1971. It was a well known landmark. Otherwise only the Three Howes, (prehistoric burial mounds) give the direction to Rosedale from the south. The Beggars' Track (p12) continues as a hollow-way past them on the south to make towards Ainhowe (Onehowe) Cross at SE 724937. This cross is a replacement for one that fell down in the 19th century; the old one is in the crypt of Lastingham Church. A track still in use goes to the latter church and village. Further south-east is Redman Cross (base only, the shaft has gone). It probably stood on a cross way of the Beggars' Track continuation to Askew and Cropton- Pickering. Now there are only hollow bulldozed tracks. They pass several shallow quarry pits called 'Glass Holes" but the glass furnace was much further down on the side of Rosedale West. They were for obtaining siliceous sand for glass smelting (120).

At Rosedale Bank Top were several calcining kilns for roasting iron-ore from Hollins Mine. Some remain, but the engine house has gone, its stones used for building Hutton Village Hall in 1938 (121). The trod continues (in parts only) down the very steep (1 in 3) bank to the Village of Rosedale Abbey.

ROSEDALE

Rosedale Abbey (actually a priory) was almost all gone by the end of the mining era. Flagged trods lead from the village by Millstreet to White Bridge, through a large caravan park (where the trod has been destroyed recently), and up the slope to the west to Hobb Farm. They continue to Thorgill House and in places on the side of Daleside Road to Hall Farm, a much renovated 17th century house, by Powley Mires (paving at SE 704970) to High House and Moorlands Farm (rebuilt in 1748) above Millfield Bridge (SE 695989).

Two paved trods joined here and one went through the cross passage of the old house. Local tradition has it that the door of the passage should never be locked. One night about midnight there was a loud knocking on the door, inadvertently locked by a farm hand. On opening it there stood an old woman with her leather apron full of stones. "Open t'dear ah' want to repair t'causey" she said (122). When they built the new house (still inhabited) they made the old one into a byre and left the trod in the garden.

From Millfield Bridge a lane to Rosedale East is called Battling Hill Lane. In 1550 the name was Battlin Brig Hill, possibly a recollection of the Scottish raids in the 14th century when the Priory was damaged. The trod from Moorlands over the bridge would connect with the George Cap Causeway (p19).

Part of a paved path further down the valley was ploughed up below Hill Houses, marked on old 6" maps as a footpath leading to Thorgill Bridge (SE 710968). It is joined by another from Low Bell End, to the east.

Another paved trod leads from Rosedale Abbey to Heygate, on the west side of the present road. Heygate Farm was a former cruck house converted to a byre. A stone found in the garden may record a Peirson.

P
I: R
1756

There are also two stretches of trod in Northdale, near Northdale Farm. Further south, a trod still exists in part under the verge of the track south-east of the White Horse Inn (SE 725955) to Hollins Farm.

ROSEDALE - HAMER

The Heygate Bankroad climbing out of Rosedale towards the Hancow branch (SE 739966) to Hartoft and also on to Egton is certainly medieval. In 1327-8 Robert de Stuteville gave "the Vale of Rossedale as far south as Anchow (Hancow) by the high road lying by Anchow as far as Syene" (Seven) (123). Sewell (124) claims that the Hamer road to Rosedale Abbey was the principal route from Whitby to the south-west in medieval times. But his evidence, based on a lead token found in Rosedale used as a passport by travellers between the two religious houses of Whitby and Rosedale is very insubstantial.

From Heygate Bank (950ft), the road passes over Brown Hill, another of many so called on the North York Moors (see p15) to Hamer Bridge, by the medieval sheep house enclosure at SE 742977, still walled in parts, (120 yards by 800). Over Crook Beck Rigg 950ft at 1075ft is Hamer House, now almost gone but formerly the Lettered Board Inn, a refreshment stop for travellers, especially thirsty lime carriers. Old folk remembered rows of lime wagons waiting here while the drivers drank ale and watered the horses from a well by the road. Most of the lime traffic took place in the late 18th to mid 19th centuries (125). As at Blakey, much coal was obtained near Hamer. The outlines of many tip-heaps can still be seen especially to the west of the ruin. Other foundations can be traced on the west side of the road just north of Hamer. One is called Gibson House on the 1855 map. The turf walls of its fields can be traced.

HAMER - GLAISDALE

The road now descends to Bluewath or Blawwath Beck, mentioned in the 13th century. Here it branched, to the north-west, by Flat Howe. From here several tracks lead to Bluewath Peat Holes, still in use for Glaisdale district. It was here whilst digging peat in 1912 that a hoard of thirty 3rd century Roman coins was found, by a peat cutter Mr Tindall of Moorsholm. About half of them were 'barbarous' imitations of radiate coins of the late 270 AD (118). It was appropriate that he should find them because they were lost by a native Romano-British peat cutter over 1600 years previously.

On the same slope to the north-west is Peat Hill 1300ft also known as Cock Heads, marked by a large walled cairn possibly Bronze Age, and a ringcairn. Dr. Elgee says "close to Stonegate and Fryup Street are the remains of narrow stone-flagged causeways, so common on the moors. Fryup Street continues as George Cap Causeway to the head of the dale (see p19). It passes close by Cock Heads. From here can be seen Huntcliff, Goldsborough, Whitby, Cawthorn, Malton and even York. A beacon on Cock Heads could flash the news of a Saxon invasion from the coast to the capital instantaneously" (54). It is doubtful if York can be seen from Cock Heads because of intervening high ground (almost 1350ft) even if the air was clear. A beacon was lit here in later times but only to give warning to the Whitby area.

The Lealholm road, called Yarlesgate, skirts the head of Glaisdale. Two standing stones on the south-west side at NZ 736014, are part of a number erected by a local road surveyor Thomas Harwood, about 1735 (see Appendix G). Other stones stand by the road (waymarkers) and lower down is the Grey Mare and the York Stone, the latter with dates of boundary perambulations. Further on at 1174ft (NZ 733017) is a culvert with an interesting name, Pannierman Brigstone.

A track from Glaisdale Head Park and Midge Hall comes in from the north-east a short distance away. This road, only recently metalled, comes in from Glaisdale to Caper Hill, the continuation of the Common Loning, a lane, referred to as 'les laundes' in a medieval French document of 1431-2. Thomas Harwood (Appendix G) inscribed a stone built into a wall 'FIRST DRAFT WAY MADE UP ALL THE COMMON LONING IN 1699'. This gives a date when the hollow-way was widened for wagons. At the junction at 1186ft (NZ 732022) stands another of Harwood's stones, this time dated 1735, a way marker inscribed - Peat Hill road, Glaisdale road, Kirby road, and Whitby road.

The road goes gently downhill into a slack. On the east side stands the Rokan Stone (NZ 730029) whose name has long been a puzzle but it may be from Old Norse for Raven. In the slack are remains of an unrecorded cross-ridge earthwork, a portion left with the Hart Leap Stones on top 40ft apart. The usual legend of the hart pursued by a hound that gave a last death leap of 40ft is marked by these stones. More likely they are part of a device for herding the deer. The bank and ditch from NZ 735035 to 736035 are certainly the remains of an earthwork similar to those on Danby Rigg and elsewhere.

To the south above High Dale or Hardhill several bell-pits for the mining of iron ore are visible, and at Red House (now a barn) are large slag heaps from iron working. The road goes up Hartleap Bank and down to Bainley Bank (14th century Bainwithlythe) where it is joined by the continuation of the George Gap Way (p19). A plain uninscribed stone shaft 4ft high on a 3ft wide base socket marks the junction.

A paved footpath runs the entire length of the west side of Glaisdale, from near the school (NZ 772052) to Midge Hall (NZ 744021) with a date stone of 1690 on the lintel. The path has been restored in places. The hillside west of Midge Hall is called 'The Park' and above this is a large roughly circular enclosure, but nothing is known of its purpose. There is no trace of paving before Midge Hall, though a path leads down to the beck. On the east side of the beck was a notable ruin (now demolished) Rigg House. It was a small cottage 32ft by 18ft, one pair of crucks and salt box, but the unusual feature was the massive upright slabs of the lintel, forming the only doorway. It had affinities with the door jambs of some Anglo-Saxon churches (126).

Further down the dale the paved trod passes Yew Grange. There are more examples of old type dwellings. Postgate Farm (NZ 758043) has a fine witch post, with two St. Andrew's crosses and a floral motif. It was found re-used as a lintel over the door of an earth closet; now the post is in the farmhouse. It is dated 1664 and marked EP JB (127).

Below Postgate stood Plum Tree (1659) now rebuilt, and on the hillside to the west was a medieval bloomery furnace excavated by the late George Harland, probably in use around the 13-14th century. A paved trod may have led from this site into the dale where paving can be traced over the beck towards New House.

Further down the dale is Quarry Farm (NZ 769047), a much altered long-house which contains a fine witch post with another "St. Andrew's Cross" (128). Nearby is Red House, from which a trod runs winding down to the beck and to old workings at NZ 775 044. Whether these are for ironstone or jet is uncertain. Just off the dale side road to the east is Hart Hall (NZ 774049). Date on south-east front TC 1684; 1790 on north-east end. It has re-used crucks in loft. This is the site of the famous Hob in Atkinson's story who turned his hand to all kinds of hard labour for the farmer. But when given some clothing he exclaimed, "Gin Hob mun hae nowght but a hardin 'hamp, He'll come nae mair, nowther te berry or stamp". A 'hardin hamp' was a coarse, sacking apron. Berry meant to thresh, stamp was used for knocking awns (ears) of barley (129).

HAMER - EGTON (YARLESGATE)

The north-eastern branch of the road from Bluewath Beck (p38) passes over Yarlsey Hill 1025ft, which may be the Yarlesgate of the medieval records. Certainly pottery of that period has been found here (130).

Yarlsey Moss lies to the east, where there is a short length of stone paving 2-3ft wide, possibly a track to the peat cuttings. On the north-west lies Wintergill, a ruin with a few small intakes and remains of coal mining and earlier iron working. Two medieval sherds were found here. Egton High Moor and Pike Hill lie to the east (tumuli and cairns here). Apart from a narrow band of higher ground the area is boggy and trackless; though from Upper Heads to Brown Hill at NZ 78/12 015-6, there are multiple deep hollow-ways, joined by others from Black Pits, north of Collier Gill crossing the Stape-Egton Road on Murk Mire Moor.

Our road crosses Wain Hill, (NZ 764022) where a track from High Gill Beck, Glaisdale, joins it. The main road turns north-east to descend the ridge between Glaisdale and Egton Grange, a lonely shallow valley once part of Budir or Butter Park (131). After passing Dog Howe (tumulus) it cuts through two cross-ridge dikes and a large cairn, William Howe (NZ 778037). This cairn was badly eroded for road metal when dug by Rev. W. Greenwell in the mid 19th century. He found a food vessel and urns (mid Bronze Age date). Formerly there were many small cairns down the slope to iron pits called the Delves, which means the 'diggings' as in the nursery rhyme: 'eleven, twelve, dig and delve'. Nearby are the Holey Intake Pits for ironstone, some still visible, 10ft deep 6ft wide. Large slag heaps here were used for road mending. Delves House is one of the few remaining examples of the 18th century cruck house left in the district, still retaining its witch post. The road winds steeply down to a ford below the junction of the Arncliffe Woods - Beggar's Bridge pannierway (p21).

In Egton Bridge paving forming footpaths can be seen towards the bridge. The old bridge was washed down in July 1930, and the present metal girder structure replaces it. A flagged path runs on the side of the present road up to Egton village. This has been restored several times. For the trod up Hill Wood to Causeway Howes see p22.

An old track went down from Glaisdale to Rakes Bridge (NZ 777067), which is mentioned in an undated extract from the County Record Office of the 17th or 18th century. "A footbridge of wood called Raike Bridge laid across the River Esk - this bridge had been built or repaired by ye inhabitants of Glaisdale. The Chapel of Glaisdale is about one mile south of this bridge and the inhabitants on the north side are pushing to have this bridge made into a horse-bridge. It is not intended for such, but they want to lay stone flaggs thereon, making it passable for horses".

The same document states that there is another road or walkstead four hundred yards below - "this is by far a greater road or thorough fair - a road to Whitby market for part of Fryup and Rosedale as well as great part of Glaisdale". It goes on to argue against the conversion of the Raike Bridge and whether the freeholders etc. can throw the "flaggs off the bridge without exposing themselves to an action at Law?"

John Davison of Lealholm did not think the work was ever carried out. The Parish Constable's Accounts for the early 1700s show that the bridge was repaired almost every year and re-laid every fifth year, certainly in 1725 and 1735. It was washed away once or twice in Mr. Davison's time and he had seen a horse go over it (132).

NORTH & WEST OF KIRKBYMOORSIDE
THURKILSTI (WELBURN - SKIPLAM - BRANSDALE RIDGE - TURKEY NAB - BATTERSBY)

Thurkilsti or Thurkil's Hill Road is one of the four important trackways over the moors near Helmsley mentioned in Walter Espec's second grant of land to Rievaulx Abbey in 1145 AD (133). It still remains in parts in its medieval state, though from Stump Cross to the Round Hill (Burton Howe) it has been levelled as a shooting track.

Its southern end is doubtful but it could have begun at York then come via Greystoke or Henderskelfe Castle (now Castle Howard). It definitely passes Thurkle Wood south-west of Sunley Cote and Sunley Hill (SE 682827), referred to as Sunnolf's Haugr (Howe) in the 12th century Rievaulx Charters, 126). Here the road is called Walcarlagate, (the road of the Britons or Churls). There are traces of the lost village of Walton or Waleton known to exist in 1086. Parker (134) mentions Roman finds here and the base of a Mortarium was given to the Ryedale Folk Museum (135). At Welburn Hall the line follows a footpath still marked by hunting gates, to the Kirkdale road which it crosses at SE 680855, also visible on RAF air photos flown in 1946 (136). If follows the modern lane called Skiplam Road past Lund Court and Skiplam Grange, one of the important Rievaulx farms to which the last Abbot retired. Roman coins were found in the vicinity, though Parker says they were from a Quarry near Wethercote (127). Rising gradually to 800ft on the limestone ridge, it is called Aldgate. At SE 643901 it is marked by a tumulus; nearby is another in Pinderdale Wood in which jet ornaments were found (137).

From the top of Skiplam Nab it descends Roll or Rowlgate Bank onto the Hagg Common, moorland until ploughed out recently. Before this ploughing the Thurkilsti at SE 627913 was a raised track some 2ft wide and 3ft high, very like a Roman road (Plate 116). Here several tracks diverge, the present one keeps on the dry ridge but the earlier one is lost in a bog. In this bog at SE 626922 stands a very weathered guide stone. On its east side is written THIS IS THE WAY TO STOKESLEY; south side, the way to KIRBY; north, THIS TO GUIS--BO (ro), and west, THIS IS THE WAY TO BILSDALE. At SE 624923, a few hundred metres north-west is the Hanging Stone, probably formerly the Lawton Stone. Many hollow-ways turn east-north-east at the guide stone, some making towards Mitchell Hagg to a very large slag heap at SE 624923 with footings of a dwelling on the west side. Two fragments of green- glazed pottery were found here. Cinder Hill, as this site was called, belonged to Stork House Bransdale. Old coal pits are found here also. A stone called Heard or Hare Chest stands at SE 617940 on the slope of Lambfold Hill (1000ft).

Before this hill is ascended note multiple tracks, at least 25 of them running parallel to the Thurkilsti, mainly on the east side. They show on air photos taken by the RAF in the late 1940s.

On the west is the shallow valley of Bonfield Gill, with more traces of probably medieval iron working at Cinderhill Wath near a slag heap, 15ft diameter. The Nawton watercourse runs on the east side of the gill, but is now silted up. It was made about 1750 by Joseph Foord (138) and crossed Bonfield Gill by a stone aqueduct with a wooden trough.

Just north of Lambfold Hill the deep hollow-way of the Thurkilsti is crossed by the modern road from Helmsley and Carlton to Bransdale (SE 613952). For about a mile ahead it follows the modern road and runs straight before turning down into Bransdale. The boundary stones are on the west side of the road, Wiley Stoup and Locking Stone, Locker Stone, described as a "great cragg" in 1829. Close to the west side of the road is a good example of the guide stones set up in 1712, inscribed - TO STOXLA (N) THIS KIRBY ROAD (E) south - TH ------- (Unfinished?) -

HELMSLEY ROAD (W) 1712. (Plate 13).

At 1199ft the Bransdale road branches north-east. The Thurkilsti continues due north on Bransdale Ridge with the boundary stones and a series of cairns, marked Tumuli on the maps. One is 53 by 17ft to 25ft wide and 3-4ft high, others are round, one with a huge stone slab on top. The views over Bransdale are superb, to the south and east the Howardian Hills and the Wolds form the horizon.

At Stump Cross (SE 607982), only the massive base and a piece of a shaft remain, though in 1829 it was called Cross With The Hand. It marks the junction of four ways, one leading down to Colt House in Bransdale (marked by a cairn).

A short distance to the north-west the Thurkilsti was joined by the MAGNA VIA (p43) "the great road coming from the Thurkilsti" as it was called in 1145 AD. At 1380ft the track to William Beck in Bilsdale branches west, still in use as a modern footpath and a shooters' road. Very little trace of the line of the Magna Via remains.

A mile north-north-west is Crookstaff Hill (139) and at NZ 605004, is the Badger Stone, a natural rock which is mentioned in Espec's charter of 1145 AD. There are only faint traces of a hollow track here. In later times the main route went to the west directly to the Round Hill on Botton Head 1489ft, the highest point of the North York Moors. The route taken from the Badger Stone probably went northwards over Badger Gill on to Cockayne Ridge joining a paved trod at the Red Stone (NZ 606015).

This east-west paved trod was called the "Street Way" in 1642. It had run from Bloworth Bridge (NZ 617014) to Hagg's Gate (NZ 573033) and Clay Bank at the head of Bilsdale. Much of this trod was damaged by bulldozing during the great fire on Urra Moor in 1961. A portion remained at NZ 605016. The stones were 3ft 6ins by 1ft 6ins and 8-9ins thick, others were smaller the larger ones were worn.

Returning to the "streetway" above, 300 yards south-east of the Round Hill, it is marked by the Face Stone Cross, (1642). This is a standing stone (NZ 597015), at 1472ft OD, with a crude weathered face, of 'Celtic type' according to some opinions. It stands at the junction of the county and district boundary. Tracks diverge towards Broad Ings and Bilsdale Head. On the side of the latter is a waymarker inscribed (west) TO INGELBY AND STOXLEY, (south) TO KIRBY AND HELMSLEY, (east) TO GISBORO, (north) with crude outstretched hand. On the main track about 100 yards south of the Round Hill is the Hand Stone (NZ 597015). "This is the way to KIRBY" and (broken off here), crude hand in relief above pointing east. On north side "THIS IS THE WAY TO STOXLA". (Plate 14)

The Thurkilsti swings north-east to Jenny Bradley on the Rudland Rigg road (p46). This stone, Jenny Bradley (NZ 611022 at 1397ft OD.) is a squat shaft in a base stone, with the 1888 boundary stone alongside her. (Plate 15)

The road follows closely the western edge of the Cleveland Hills passing the Botton or Burton Howes (NZ 608033), Bronze Age burial mounds of turf, excavated by R.S. Close, though previously disturbed (140). Prof. G.W. Dimbleby described the results of his pollen analysis of them in *The Ancient Forest of Blackamore* (30). It is difficult to realise these mounds of turf were raised in clearings of a dense forest.

Here the Ingleby coal road from the pits at Black Hagg Beck to the east worked in the early 19th century joins the rigg road (141). The Ingleby coal road and the track called the Flagged Road are shown on the old 6" maps of the area. (The latter is also on the modern maps). Rowland Close was told of pannier traffic on these roads remembered by an old man called Chapman, who said the panniermen called at Dundale Beck Farm for provisions, early in the 19th century. Close said the 'flagged' road was never paved to his recollection; it took its name from the 'flags' or rushes as at Busco Beck (p19). The coal mines were well organised as is indicated by two shafts over 106ft in depth. The mining continued for some years as it indicated by the establishment of the pannier-men's tracks. The period of activity was from late 18th to early 19th centuries.

The descent to Battersby Bank follows zig-zags from NZ 599062. It is joined by several footpaths. The local name for this bank is Turkey Nab. Mr. R.B. Turton (142) was one of the first to make the deduction that it is derived from Thurkilsti Nab. He names three Thurkylls, one in the Anglo Saxon Chronicle in 915 AD; another Thurkyll, a jarl who landed in 1069 and plundered York, and Thorkyll de Cliveland who is mentioned in the Whitby Cartulary.

Another possible route of the Thurkilsti was down a track still in use branching near a small tumulus at NZ 586023, to descend Jackson's Bank (NZ 588/9 022-050) going down 725ft to Clogger's Hall (NZ 589033). At NZ 588031 the paved trod was disturbed by forestry ploughing in 1962. Under one of the flags was a footring base of a post-medieval jar with traces of brown glaze on smooth orange ware, probably 16th-17th century. (Fig 5).

Further down on Plane Hill the trod passed round a slag heap, (at NZ 586033) where, with permission of the farmer, Mr. Grimstone, and help from Bill Cowley and Rowland Close, we excavated in 1962 part of a medieval iron-smelting hearth. It was circular, and produced a few 13-14th century sherds. South-west of Midnight House (NZ 588036) we excavated two sections of the paved causeway here 10ft wide, laid on clay, a single layer of stone slabs. It appeared to go from Midnight Farm to Plane Hill (NZ 586033). It went up Jackson's Bank, which is riddled with old jet workings and could have been laid for their transport. Jackson's Bank led to Urra Moor to meet other tracks and roads. R.B. Turton thought the Thurkilsti could have branched this way (143).

The forestry plantations have now covered most of this area. We were fortunate to obtain the evidence in 1962. A stone axe of neolithic type was found here but broken by children. Another (in the Ryedale Folk Museum) came from the foot of Ingleby Incline.

MAGNA VIA (HELMSLEY - ROPPA - BILSDALE MOOR)

This important ancient road, like Thurkilsti mentioned in Espec's 1145 grant of land (p41), left Helmsley by Baxton's Sprunt on the dry limestone ridge passing the Baxtons Farms. Roman pottery was found on the surface here by A.L Pacitto. The road goes almost due north to Roppa Edge. Roppa is derived from Rauthe (meaning red) Path and is mentioned in the Rievaulx Charters dated 1160.

On Helmsley Moor (1050ft) it slants down to meet a branch to Rievaulx, which may have descended by Harriet Air Farm (SE 575855) a curious name; R.W. Crosland thought it was derived from Norman French 'arriere terre' or Backland.

The track now a footpath joined the present Bilsdale Road at the third milestone from Helmsley. At Snilegate Head, (SE 568882) the Rievaulx road turns north-east to join the main Magna Via at the foot of Roppa Bank.

From Roppa Bank another branch goes north-east to Potter House (SE 592917, a post-medieval pottery kiln) and on to Piethorn (old coal pits). The main road went over Carr Cote Ridge passing west of a cross base, Roppa Cross at SE 588923; though 700 yards north at SE 587930 is another base marked on the map as Standing Stone. On the high ground (1000ft) to the west is a large shaft called Hanging Stone, possibly because it is leaning almost to the ground. The present track crosses Limestone Ridge by an old kiln, and goes down into Bilsdale near Crosset. The Magna Via must have curved north-east towards Basin Howe (NZ 596949) a mutilated cairn about 40ft diameter. The Magna Via forms a township (parish) boundary along this stretch. The moor is crossed by no less than nine hollow-tracks running north-north-east towards Money Howe, another cairn also damaged. The road followed a ridge less than a mile in width with Smiddales on the west and

Bonfield Gill on the east. On the ridge are the Water Stones, natural boulders - possibly here are the Bacheler Stones of the charter. Crossing onto Bilsdale Moor it would have to curve onto high ground to avoid the Swang and Black Holes bogs. Somewhere just north of Stump Cross (SE 607982) it joined the Thurkilsti, (see p41) and followed it northwards.

HELMSLEY - LASKILL - CARLTON IN CLEVELAND

It is more difficult to trace the route of another road mentioned in the Rievaulx Charters, "the Great Road which comes from Wideris". Wetherhouse (SE 554943), is the obvious choice as it is still pronounced "Wideris". But J. McDonnell says "there is no sign and little real likelihood of a Magna Via ever having passed that way. There is a road sloping up from Laskill on to the moor top, via the former grange of Low Weathercote, which passes within half a mile of Wether House. But there seems no conceivable use for such a road at that time". (144)

There is a small portion of paved trod east of Laskill at Collier Loanin. (SE 566908) It is near the Friend's Meeting House and appears to go up towards the site of Rosy Dike, a demolished cruck house.

There are a number of reasons for the existence of an east-west road. Laskill and Woolhouse Croft (SE 562914) formed part of the great Rievaulx sheep ranch. The Rievaulx tilery was situated in High and Low Kiln fields (SE 652930). There are many old coal pits at SE 559930. At SE 561930 are about sixty bell-pits of old iron-workings. There is a large embanked enclosure on Wetherhouse Moor and others at the head of Fangdale Beck. Presumably these had branch tracks leading to the road mentioned in the Rievaulx Charter (145) - "the road that goes from Halmbi (Hawnby) to Cleveland". (see Appendix B)

Several well marked tracks go from Hawnby Moor Gate (SE 540917), following the ridge north by Round Hill tumulus and by the intakes of High and Low Thwaits (shown on Robinson's map of 1818). They continue by Hob Stone to Meggy Mires and Stumpstone (on boundary) by a tumulus called Wades Hut and Arnsgill Head and Spring (SE 535981). The 1642 boundary perambulation of the Duncombe Estate (146) describes a route "Along a street way to a heap of stones at Arnsgill Head and another line of street to Meggy Mires". This route passes close to another Wetherhill at 1300ft (SE 543980) to Benky or Venty (Venter) Hill, (SE 530993), mentioned in the 1637 perambulation of Bilsdale Kirkham (146). This name, Venter, could be derived from Celtic 'Market Hill'. Fairs and markets were held on such places in the past as at Blakey Bank Top, where sheep sales are still held.

On this boundary was a "rook or heap of stones on the ancient road called Helmsley Street", mentioned in a perambulation of the Duncombe Estates in 1825. One of the stones is inscribed I.M. 1772, at Green Howe (SE 538988).

The road now follows the narrow Barker's Ridge between Raisdale and Scugdale onto Stony Wicks (NZ 528003), called Feather Codds in 1637, thence on to Carlton Bank and down into Cleveland. At NZ 522019 it is joined by another track turning westwards onto Live Moor and going down through old jet workings above Faceby Plantation by a deep hollow-way. To the south by a large stony cairn is a field system with walling and cairns, and on the end of the knoll at NZ 504009 are the ditches of an enclosure of Iron Age type found by D. Smith.

INGLEBY GREENHOW AREA

A paved trod noted by R.S. Close and Alec Wright followed the line of a footpath south-west of Battersby at NZ 593072. It turns sharply south to a stone on the north side of the modern road to Ingleby Greenhow towards Stone Stoup Hill. There is a branch on the south-west side of Bank Foot. This went to Ingleby Manor and crossing the beck through the plantations joined another trod turning to Folly Farm and Howe Hill. Other lengths were visible in 1970, south of Low Farm (NZ 585050), and south of Wood's Farm (NZ 589046) through Pig Park towards the vicarage where a guide stone of 1711 vintage remains. This line leads to Woods Farm (NZ 589046) and a trod at Midnight Farm. Ingleby Greenhow was the Camisedale of Domesday Book (147). There is a footpath west of the avenue by the 1711 guide stone near the vicarage. On the corner of Church Lane a paved trod turns due south to Folly Farm and How Hill, thence towards Jackson's Bank.

BILSDALE AND RAISDALE

In The History of Helmsley (148) it is stated - "Even 800 years ago there was no road along the bottom of Bilsdale. Such settlers as had penetrated into the dale lived higher up the flanks, along the spring line and they made contact with the outside world by climbing up to the ridgeways which skirted the east and west sides". Since that was written in 1963 we have gathered more information. Chop Gate is said to take its name from Old Scandinavian 'Kaup' in old English 'Cheap' meaning a 'pedlar' or 'packman', although there is some doubt about this. In the Middle Ages the hamlet of Chop Gate may have been a trading post or market on a pedlar's or pannierman's road. Since no road ran up the dale bottom it must have crossed it, probably from the Urra Moor pannier way and the William Beck track, the branch of the Magna Via and the Thurkilsti.

The road running through Raisdale near the mill is called 'Red Way', this is some distance from the Red Road mentioned in the charters (Appendix B). The present road continues on the east slope of Wath Hill which blocks this part of Raisdale, rising to 1000ft. John McDonnell suggested it might be the site of a pele tower; a Johannes del Pele is named in Bilsdale in the Lay Subsidy of 1301. The road climbs steadily to 975ft at Three Lord's Stone (NZ 523030), before descending steeply down Carlton Bank. Much alum and jet was obtained here. There are extensive views into Cleveland.

South of Raisdale is High Crosslets Farm (NZ 536003), reached by a pannierway from Scugdale Hall (NZ 518000).

From Chop Gate, an old lane climbs north onto Cold Moor north-west of Chop Hill from SE 558998. It runs between stone walls into a deep hollow-way marked as a footpath on the 6" map before dividing into three paths. One following the ridge turns north by the Three Howes and down to Broughton via the Bank Lane. It passes through the Garfitt Gap below the Wain Stones, eroded gritstone crags much beloved by rock climbers. At 800ft stands the isolated small holding of Whingroves, home of Arthur Denick Frankland who has given us some useful information on the area. The second path descends to Beak Hills (NZ 548023) in the pass leading up to Donna Cross at NZ 545034, mentioned by Elgee but not shown on the later OS maps. Southwards the pass leads by a boggy valley below Beak Hills to Hall Garth and High Clay House, survivals of a possible medieval hamlet. A scatter of pottery and a quern base point to occupation in the 13th-14th century (149).

The third track runs on the south end of Cold Moor by Round Hill, High West Cote and Stone Intake to the Red Way and Raisdale Mill. Alec Wright said this was partly paved in the past. It is rather a surprise to find a substantial mill in this tiny dale, over 700-900ft O.D. The three storey mill was erected by John Garbutt in 1849. A later John Garbutt ran it until 1920. Now it houses cattle, and there are few arable fields in the vicinity.

Above Urra is a remarkable earthwork running for two and a half miles to a point east of William Beck Farm (SE 569994). The bank is 12ft wide and 5ft high with stone revetted on the west side over a ditch. It is likely to be medieval. There is a grant by Simon de Ver to Kirkham Abbey the "chapel of Bilsdale with all his land outside his bank 'defensa' next his hall southwards to William Beck". It was called Cliff Dyke in 1642. The descent to Clay Bank was called Cliff Ditch in 1637.

WAINGATE - RUDLAND RIGG ROAD
(KIRKBYMOORSIDE - FADMOOR - RUDLAND RIGG - BATTERSBY BANK)

The alternative route to the Magna Via and Thurkilsti was Waingate (from Kirkbymoorside) and on to Rudland Rigg. The southern end starts at Kirkbymoorside Market Place, already important by 1276 AD. As late as the early 20th century it had a beast, horse and swine market. Drovers still existed in 1930 and William Carter of the iron foundry remembered droves of ponies and donkeys standing there in 1880-90. Joe Dowson of Kirkbymoorside drove a wagonette over to Stokesley and Kendrew of Easby came weekly for butter and eggs in a covered wagon. Even then the purely moorland section from Rudland to Battersby was very rough. It has never been tarred beyond Bransdale junction above Rudland. This stretch gives the conditions of medieval roads. Nor was there a single inn for twelve miles apart from the Hope Inn at Rudland which closed early this century and is now a cottage.

From Kirkbymoorside a limestone road in the 19th - early 20th century went up on the side of the Manor Vale, site of Neville Castle demolished in the 17th century. The road forks at Creaking Howe (SE 683882), on the right to Gillamoor, on the left to Fadmoor, by Bitterdale Lane and Onams Lane, by three quarries. Fadmoor (SE 674893) has a nice green and the Plough Inn.

The lane leading north from Fadmoor was called Waingate from Anglo-Saxon - Waen Way or Waggon Road. It leads onto the edge of the limestone hills at Boonhill, 800ft, where many old tracks show on air-photos. At SE 668909 part of a bronze-founders hoard was ploughed up at different times between 1966 and 1975. There were five broken socketed bronze axes and pieces of a sword and spear, all dating to about 700-1000 BC. Highfield Lane from Gillamoor joins the Waingate here. Descending Fadmoor Bank there are fine views to the north and east and of the pit-hills on the old Rudland coalfield. Hope Inn Farm (SE 663917) retains the name of the inn though no longer its licence. The late Adam Gordon, Lord Feversham's game keeper, remembered having drinks here in 1914; "poor beer and only two customers". In the heyday of lime leading, the mid 19th century, it had many more, as it was a long dusty drive or walk to the next one in Cleveland. Past a Methodist chapel closed by 1965 and a few scattered small-holdings it crosses one of the longest stretches of uninhabited moorland in North East Yorkshire. From now on it is unsurfaced. There is a series of oolitic moor-coal pits in rows on both sides of the road, worked from the early 17th century (or before) to 1912 (150).

Two miner's cottages, Siccason and Rose Cottage, survived until the 20th century, but are now only ruins. There are not many tumuli in contrast to the other ridge roads, though he mis-named Hobtrusch Rook (SE 661945) lies a short distance to the east, it is a damaged stone cairn about 45ft wide with two concentric kerbs. When opened a cist was found but was empty, either robbed earlier or the burial had perished (151). A waymarker by the road called Willey Stoup is inscribed KIRBY RODE.

At SE 654949 on a hollow-way leading into Farndale is another waymarker, inscribed THIS KERBY RAD, and on the north side THIS PICKERING ROAD - STOXLY ROAD. This track leads east down Mill Bank and Plumpton by Low Mill to climb the Sprunt to Blakey Rigg and the Beggars' Track (p12). Other eastward tracks go down Double Crag to Scarth Nick (ironworkings and jet). (Plate 16)

At West Gill Head at SE 641975, the Rudland Rigg road crosses that from Farndale up Monket Bank to Bransdale (p47). Nearby are the Three Howes at Ousegill Head. These howes contained cremation urns of the Bronze Age. A further track to Farndale runs north-east at 1245ft to Penny Hill Crag (Pen - Celtic for hill or howe), where there were jet workings and a deep hollow-way to Duffinstone (NZ

647988) the Duvanasthwaite of the Rievaulx Charter. The stone still remains but was cut into when work was being done on the Farndale West road. Duffin is from old Celtic Dubh - Dark, thwaite means clearing near the stone.

At 1330ft another track from Bransdale joined the Rigg Road - now levelled into a forestry road with a waymarker, Cockan Cross, by it at SE 632991. This stone is inscribed on the sides STOXL RODE, KIRBY RODE, FARNDALE RD and BRANSDALE RODE. It is damaged and has a broken shaft in a socket.

At Cockan Cross, a branch track from Shaw Ridge joins Rudland Rigg and runs parallel with the Rigg Road though turning due south by the Three Howes and a large moor coal pit all on the 1300ft ridge. 'Shaw' denotes woodland, although trees have long vanished here. The track is mentioned in documents from 1282 and is still visible although now disused. This track crossed the Farndale-Bransdale road near quarries south-west of Ousegill Head. At 1125ft a knoll (SE 635963) is called Anzit Howe by the locals but not so named on the 6" map. Another east-west track crosses Black Wath on Ouse Gill; several hollow-ways here and more towards Spout House in Bransdale. Further down Ousegill near a sheep-fold to the east of the beck are several old walled fields or intakes, but no date can be fixed on them. They are clear on RAF air photos (152). A weir is marked on the map, but this may be for a water course of the Foord type 1750 (153).

At 1314ft is a really ancient boulder set up on the east side of the rigg road, the Cammon Stone from the Celtic 'cam' meaning bank stone. On its leaning side is a Hebrew inscription HALLELUJAH. (Plate 17). This was the source of much controversy. It was though to be Phoenician but can be compared with the Hebrew lettering on Bransdale Mill inscription. It is most likely the work of Rev. W. Strickland, a 19th century Vicar of Ingleby. R.S. Close said there were two other stones inscribed in Hebrew on Turkey Nab to which the Rudland Rigg road leads. They were destroyed and used to mend the road. From this stone the road climbs to its highest point, 1330ft, descending gradually to Bloworth Bridge where it was crossed by the dismantled mineral railway from Rosedale. The crossing house was the only building between Rudland and Battersby Incline Foot. It was only built about 1860 and destroyed by the army in 1943-4. The road then joins Thurkilsti at Jenny Bradley (NZ 612023) and passes northwards to Battersby Bank.

FARNDALE - MONKET BANK - BRANSDALE

A short length of paving stones runs in Farndale from Middle Heads (NZ 632009) to Elm House (NZ 642003) in Farndale mostly near the latter. There were flags at Long Causeway House further down the dale (SE 653991), though not many flags remain since being re-set in 1964. Flags also exist considerably further south, at Ewecote Farm (SE 682938). A paved trod from the foot of Blakey Bank (SE 673978), continues in parts past North Gill House and the old cruck house, rebuilt in 1908. The trod turns sharply north-east to the moor below the Pannierman's Seaves and spring (SE 680991, p12), where there are traces of others from Wold House (SE 675956) towards the mill.

The road up Monket Bank linked the two dales and was used as a church way. It starts opposite Monket House (SE 661972), called Munckgate in the 14th century, climbing steeply up a deep hollow-way from 675ft to 1212ft up the side of the shale slips of Monket House Crags, up Penny Hill. Always rough, by 1985 it was very deeply rutted, some 6 to 14ins deep in parts. Only tractors could use it, and even they had to detour onto the moor to avoid the worst places. It crosses Ousegill Head and the Rudland Rigg track southwards from Cockan Cross, marked by piles of stones. On the east side of Bransdale the track divides. A deep hollow-way goes straight down to Smout House, but the main track descended more gradually, north-west by some intakes to Cow Sike House where it joined the Bransdale East road to Cockan Kirk.

This was the route used by bearers carrying the corpse of one of the Greystocks of Shotten Hill, Farndale, to Cockan Kirk in Bransdale, described to the writer by an old lady living at Scarborough, who attended the funeral in the 1870s. She also remembered an Aconley of Frost Hall carried over the rigg by a higher route that came over below Cockan Cross. These are genuine corpse roads like that over Danby Rigg described by Canon Atkinson (154). However despite the legend, the modern Lyke Wake Walk was never used as such. No bearers would carry a corpse forty miles even in relays.

In Bransdale there is a short length of paved trod south-west of the church (SE 619978 - 620979). There are also trods around the mill running down by the beck southwards and also near Catherine House (SE 619952).

THE HAMBLETON STREET

The most notable and for long the dominant of all the ancient trackways running north-south across the western end of the high moors was the Hambleton Street. It is a portion, still largely in its original condition, of a major trade artery in prehistoric times. It was referred to as a 'Regalis Via' or 'King's Way' in a document in the Rievaulx Chartulary (155).

K.L. Bonser says (156) "it is the best preserved stretch of drove road in Yorkshire, - part of a track of great antiquity, Mesolithic, Neolithic, Bronze Age, Romano-British, from the Channel to Scotland" Dr. F. Elgee calls it "the finest ridgeway in the district. It traverses the plateau from Roulston Scar to Black Hambleton, climbing from 600 to 1250ft in 15-16 miles. Along this route came long-barrow man as far north as Kepwick Moor, followed by Beaker makers, who were succeeded by the urn folk, whose round barrows mark its course" (157).

Against this view Dr. D.A. Spratt says (158) "We cannot any longer assume the Hambleton Street is Neolithic or Bronze Age. It appears to have developed some time between the use of the northern part of the dike system and 1209, when it is first mentioned as 'the road leading to Cleveland'. It may have developed in the Roman period, for there are Roman settlements in the south at Oldstead and Hood, and at the northern end at Whorlton". His theory is not backed by excavation. There is no firm evidence that the Kepwick Dike is cut by the Hambleton Street or is earlier, as he suggests.

The Hambleton Street is presumed by Bonser (156) to have crossed Northumberland and Durham to Yarm where there was held a great fair and market. From Yarm it followed the road south to Crathorne and passing west of Hutton Rudby, by Toft Hill and Black Horse Lane by Potto Hall to Black Horse Farm (formerly Drover's Inn NZ 472020) just west of Swainby. Here it began to climb the hills at Scarth Nick (NZ 473004, from the Skar(th)I, meaning gap or notch) in the Cleveland Hills, climbing 800ft in less than a mile.

Arthur Young described it in 1771 - "You are obliged to cross the moors they call Black Hambleton, over which the road runs in narrow hollows that admits a south country chaise (Cart) with some difficulty, that I reckon this part of the journey made at the hazard of my neck. The going down into Cleveland is beyond all description, terrible, you go through such steep, rough, narrow, rock precipices, that I would sincerely advise you to go a hundred miles to escape it" (159).

The ascent of the Cleveland Hills at Scarth Nick is still steep and narrow, but the surface is much improved, now all tarmac to the Sheep Wash Ford. (SE 471993). Here the Osmotherley road branches south but the Drove Road retains its primitive roughness continuing south through old intakes by High Lane past an old limekiln, to the remains of Solomon's Temple (SE 474972). This was no imposing shrine but the ruins of a house "built by one intent on retirement the world forgetting". But the old hermit, one Matt Walker, either changed his mind or ill-calculated the cost; the funds at his disposal failed, so it remains to this day a rebuke to his folly. He long held 'squatter's right possession of the place' but he died some time ago aged 90 (160).

A short distance to the south is Chequers Inn on Slapestones Ford. (SE 475970). The Inn had a chequer board sign - "Be not in haste, Step in and taste, Good Ale tomorrow for nothing". (But tomorrow never comes!) The inn was held by the Flintoffs for over 100 years. It had a turf fire said to have been kept alight for over 200 years (this legend is told of other ancient inns). Turf cakes were a speciality there, people went to eat them and partake of the home-brewed ale. It is now a private house, though not altered much outside since the turn of the century. From the Chequers the road runs straight over Jenny Brewster's Moor and Oakdale Head to the steep ascent of Black Hambleton, 1275ft. Between Solomon's Temple and this point the Drove Road is surfaced, as the road from Snilesworth and Hawnby. There are old limekilns on the side and at Potters Keld (SE 479950). 'Potter' could be a personal name, or the site of a pottery kiln.

From the summit of Black Hambleton, the highest point traversed by the 'Street', magnificent views present themselves. To the west and north-west over the Vale of Mowbray the Pennines form the horizon, from Whernside to Cross Fell. In the days of steam trains plumes of smoke could be seen continually moving up or down the vale below. The road follows the edge of the escarpment past a large tumulus at point SE 481942. The highest point attained is on this section at 1280ft on Dodd End (SE 482940). Much eroded limestone on the surface gives the name Whitestone to the gill falling sharply onto Kepwick Moor. The Street again turns due south by a series of old quarries to Limekiln House (SE 491919), now only a bare ruin though formerly a welcome place of refreshment on this high, cold and dry plateau. The drovers had a stance for their cattle, there was a continual traffic of lime, but it was also a resort for smugglers and sheep rustlers. The road from Kepwick to Arden and Hawnby is crossed below a group of large walled intakes and a boundary stone inscribed CT 1770, stands at the junction of a track leading down to Windygill Ridge on Cowesby Moor. This is another Salter Gate, marked by tumuli to Seta Pike (SE 478888), a mile to the west.

On the moor west of the street is the Long Barrow (SE 491904), constructed mainly of earth, with the fragmentary remains of five bodies near the east end. Only two flint flakes were found with them. Elgee remarks on the scarcity of associated relics, but Greenwell who dug the barrow only trenched it in a few places and never dug the surrounding ditch which might have produced artifacts (161). On the west is an interesting group of barrows, one very large round barrow with a small one close by, and to the south a large ring cairn. North-east of this group is a dike which continues on Little Moor to a series of pits. It has a branch towards the south-west. Dr. D.A. Spratt in his paper on the "Cleave Dike" (162) says "the Kepwick Dike is cut by the Hambleton Street and by the Kepwick-Hawnby road and their associated hollow-ways and thus appears to be earlier than both". But without excavation to prove this one cannot say which is earlier.

Steeple Cross (SE 495901) is simply a rough boulder marking a boundary, possibly replacing an early cross. 500 yards to the west is another boulder called Friar's Cross. Both stand on the longest east-west dike, named after Steeple Cross which ends in Stony Gill south-east of Arden Hall. This cross is named in a fine between Henry, Abbot of Byland and Nicholas de Bolteby in 1246 which mentions "the king's road that leads by the Spina de Kereby to Stepicros" (163). It is most likely that most of the dikes running up to the Hambleton Street were medieval boundaries, but only excavation could solve this problem.

From Steeple Cross a track leads west called Red Gate, by a very prominent tumulus on the 1000ft ridge, called Gallow Howe (SE 483899). Here it follows hollow tracks northwestwards onto Pen Hill where Dr. Spratt found a rectangular enclosure - now under plough (164). A very deep hollow-way leads from the side of

Pen Hill down to Kepwick.

The Hambleton Street has been eroded by the forestry plantations for over a mile southwards. The old name for the wood here was Cracoe (Celtic - Crag Wood). At Lord's Tongue (SE 503894) the Cleave Dike ran on the east side of the street but was bulldozed by the Forestry Commission in 1960. In the remains of the bank of the Cleave Dike I trowelled out two pieces of clay tobacco pipe in 1960. This dike runs for over five miles never far in from the escarpment edge; it is most likely the result of boundary and pasture disputes in the late 16th to 17th centuries.

The road and dike part company at the Hesketh Dike at SE 509878. Hesterskeid (Rievaulx Chartulary, 1153) is old Norse for Racecourse. Two miles south is the Hambleton Down racecourse on a very level piece of ground with a fall of only a few feet in its two-mile length. It was used from before 1612 to 1776 when the races were transferred to York. There are still racing stables at Hambleton.

The Hesketh Dike is another east-west cross ridge type from Moor Ings to Sneck Yate at the top of Boltby Bank. It is a massive work 40ft wide with a ditch 20ft wide and still 3ft deep possibly double in parts. At Silver Hill (SE 512878) a tumulus 60ft diameter and 6ft high seems to intrude into the bank. Both were thought by Denny (165) to be of turf construction. The portion shown on the old OS maps west of the street has been ploughed down. Here the Cleave Dike crossed it. This is a vital point for excavation to find out more of both dikes. The purpose of the dike seems to have been to regulate traffic on the road, which therefore must have been earlier.

The road from Murton and Hawnby crosses at Sneck Yate. Here stood the famous wooden guide post pointing north to Yarm and south to Malton. There were several tumuli around Silver Hill Farm. A stone cist that once contained a burial was visible in one of them and another produced a bronze spear. The track from Thirlby up Skipton Hill in a deep hollow-way at SE 505837-9 climbs from 500 to 1150ft. The footpath is by a deep hollow-way or turf road on its north side.

The street follows a very straight course southwards to Dialstone House (SE 518843). The Dial Stone is a rounded boulder inscribed 1705. W. Ness. It is certainly not a sundial. Bonser suggests it could be part of the weighing equipment used by the judges at the racecourse.

A grassy plot on Cold Kirby Moor is used as a training ground for race-horses from the Hambleton Hotel. A track to Sutton Bank crosses over the gallop but the line of the Street runs south as a green lane to join the A170. The base of Cooper's Cross is close to the modern road towards Sutton Bank Top. From the hotel the street is lost, but a line of walling marks its course, lined by old quarries to Shaw's Moor where the present road goes to Scotch Corner (SE 527813). This was the site of the surprise attack by the Scots on Edward II army at the battle of Byland in 1322 (166). Bonser says it was the site of a drovers' inn. There is a modern chapel erected here and a walled well at SE 526815. Oldstead Bank joins the road from Kilburn at Scawling Wood. Scaws was a local name for iron-slag and there is a slag heap in Cockerdale Wood one mile north-east. Nearby Roman pottery was made and Roman fields are under the forestry plantations.

Oldstead village is old, as its name suggests, and has produced Roman pottery and querns. The Black Swan Inn may have also been a drover's resort. The line of a pannier-way from Oldstead to Low Kilburn has been pointed out to me by Mr. T. Banks of Low Kilburn. It extends from the south end of Oldstead village (SE 530799) by a footpath still in use and by River Head Road to the junction (SE 521796) with River Lane and from thence into High Kilburn village and downhill to St. Mary's Vicarage. At SE 514797 it is visible as a cobbled way 3 ft wide for a short distance but is lost before reaching the ford in Kilburn village street at the junction of Butter Lane and Carr Lane. It may have gone by way of Balk, Bagby and the old bridge at Sowerby to Thirsk.

The track continues along a causeway by Scencliff Grange (SE 527793, another Roman site) and Coxwold where an old raised causeway led to Oulston and Crayke, its prominent hill crowned with church and castle. At Crayke Mrs. N. Knowles identified a former drover's inn called Wart and Dot, with a field of the same name that could have been a stance (a field into which pannier ponies were turned). From Crayke the road passed Stillington Grange to Huby and York.

The Malton branch, known as High Street, diverged via Tom Smith's Cross (SE 571812) on the modern A170 four miles east of Sutton Bank. The shaft of the cross, without a base, has been removed by the Forestry Commission to another site nearby. The original cross is mentioned in the 1642 survey (167). The road passes through the Double Dikes and Studford Ring, which was possibly an Iron Age stock enclosure. The barrows around it were dug in 1966 and produced very crude Iron Age pottery and flints. Several Bronze Age or earlier barrows lie on the line to Ampleforth Beacon (700ft). The road went by Oswaldkirk Bank Top (though possibly not by the route of the modern B1257) to Stonegrave, which has a Saxon Minster and carved stones, to Hovingham, with a Roman villa site and late Saxon Church. Then it took the Roman road to Malton or followed the ridge and earthworks to the south and joined Braygate Street to Malton.

Malton has been important since Roman times with a fort, and a medieval castle which only had a short life. The stock market and fairs developed in the Middle Ages and still survives. The numerous roads radiating from this little town may be based on the Roman road system and may have been kept alive because of the stock market (168).

HIGH STREET AND TURNGATE
(LYTHE - SCALING - COMMONDALE - KILDALE)

East-west routes such as this are much less clear than the ridge roads mainly because the rivers and dales form natural divisions. Tracks from dale to dale over the ridges are plentiful, some used as church or corpse roads, others merely access or turf roads and moor-coal roads. The Victoria County History mentions in its description of Danby (169) that "Prehistoric roads ascend from the Vale of Pickering; north of the Esk a road passed westwards along the ridge from Lythe, over Danby Moor, and
from the number of tumuli in its course, it ought to be one of the most important in the district". The same might be said of several of our ridge roads certainly of the Thurkilsti and the Pannierman's Way by Foster Howes and Lilla Howe.

West of Lythe the road is called High Street where it follows the modern A174. Although 'street' in old place names often indicates a Roman road, there is no known association here except for the fact that it goes towards the site of the Roman signal station at Goldsborough on the coast. It crosses Newton Mulgrave and Ellerby Moors with their several tumuli, Neolithic to Beaker and Bronze Age (170). Newton Mulgrave is referred to in medieval document as Newton Substrata meaning 'under the street', which may be another allusion to a Roman road. It intersects another road probably as old (see p20) east of Scaling Dam and crosses several hollow-ways at Waupley Bridge.

At High Thorn Stone (NZ 719122) it slants south-west and follows the modern road to Danby End, but at Robin Hoods Butts (the large tumulus dug by Atkinson, east of the Danby road), it is still unpaved and leads westwards between the other Robin Hood's Butts (a ring cairn) and south of Herd Howe (NZ 704118), also dug by Atkinson. It contained no less than sixteen cremations - if Atkinson found them all, which is doubtful. It was called Turngate Hill and from here that name is given to the trackway, said to be another drove road in its later years.

Turngate climbs to 850ft passing a large oval enclosure on Gerrick Moor. It then descends to a very boggy slack, Sand Wath and climbs to another 850ft hill, south-east of Job Cross (NZ 686110). This is a crude plain shaft and an earlier base. Woodwark says "the pillar is modern" (171). Traces of hollow tracks cross north-south here. The Turngate is called Mell Howe Gate here on the 1660 Danby Boundary Perambulations. White Cross with its five road junctions lies ahead. This cross is wrongly given as No 11 in Woodwark (172). The pannier trod westwards to Commondale and Thunderbush is described elsewhere in this book.

The present road to Kildale probably follows the old line by Wayworth Moor, over Sleddale intersected by the Ernaldsti at the foot of Percy Rigg. Here on the slope above Wood EndCottages (ironworker's houses, NZ 619101) is a very extensive cairn-field with hut circles and ancient plots running up to Brown Hill. Crag Bank south of the road and now a plantation, had native British huts with Roman pottery and querns. More were dug by Rowland Close further up on the slopes of Pale End. Kildale had a Viking settlement 1,000 years later. Burials of this period were found when the church was rebuilt in 1867 (173). Part of a cross-head of the same period was found in excavations on the Manor Site in 1968-75. Much medieval pottery and other artifacts came from this excavation.

The road passes through the Kildale Gap at Dundale Beck with the railway nearby and the River Leven flowing through a narrow gorge where great floods swept away a Bleach Mill and its dams about 160 years ago, although there is still a Bleach Mill Farm at NZ 596043. The Dun (NZ 589084) is undoubtedly the earthwork of Easby Castle hill, a horse-shoe shaped bank and ditch, probably erected by Bernard de Balliol, Lord of Ingleby (174). Trial trenches by R.S. Close and the writer in 1960-61 on the interior and in the shallow ditch in 1961 did not produce any evidence of occupation or date, but it could have been unfinished. The 600ft promontory on which it stands commands a very fine prospect of the Cleveland Plain below. The farm higher up the ridge at NZ 586093 is called Borough Green, suggestive of Roman occupation.

There is a branch south of Kildale, to Baysdale, where the modern road along Park Brow follows an old route. It is probably medieval, as is the bridge at Baysdale.

The Stokesley road probably followed the route used at present, going by Easby. It was called 'the old cattle road' by Sewell (175). Ingleby Greenhow lies to the south, to where the Waingate and Thurkilsti descend by the steep Turkey Nab.

Stokesley has a fine old packhorse bridge. The modern A172 road to Nunthorpe is still called Pannierman's Lane.

At Linthorpe in 1439, an ox, a quarter of wheat and a quarter of barley (for brewing beer) were provided for the funeral feast of Robert Thompson, "a pannierman" or driver of packhorses (222).

NORTH OF HAWNBY

From Blowgill near Hawnby shorter lengths of paved trods run north-west from iron working and limekilns at Streetgate Farm (SE 528933) to Hagg House and to Birk Wood Farm (SE 517940). This line runs on the 600-650 foot contour line at a lower level than the present road. There are traces of stone flags and paving at intervals. It is little used at present, with hedges on both sides; culverts remain. It could have turned north at Plane Tree Hall and followed the present road to the ford at Great Bridge Foot and been joined at Low Locker by a track from the south side of the Rye over Black Intake (large slag heap).

Another track leaves the Hawnby road 600 yards south of Streetgate Farm. It goes down to the Rye at Thack Wath, by another slag heap at SE 529922. Here a greenglazed medieval sherd was found in the heap. It continues south-south-east up to Hawnby Hill End with a branch to Moor Gate (SE 540917) where the road shown on Robinson's map of 1818 runs north over Hawnby Moor to Round Hill and the Thwaites (p44).

The Rievaulx Charter of 1170 (176) states "the boundaries between the brothers of Lauescales (Laskill?) and Bildesdale, and the brothers of Snigleswath (Snilesworth), shall be the road which leads from Halmbi to Cleveland ..." Also mentioned but dating from 1007 (177) are boundaries between Whorlton and Snilesworth, from 'Neleshou' - as the water falls - on both sides to 'Harthou' and then to 'Pundcalehou', then as the water falls to the Red Road.

SPERRAGATE (WEST OF HELMSLEY)

East-west roads through Helmsley are described in the History (178). Travelling west, Helmsley was left, not by Rye Bridge as the modern A170 here is less than a century old - but by the present Bilsdale-Stokesley Road, as far as the Scawton turning. Thence the modern by-road past Abbot's Hagg and down to Rievaulx Bridge (also known as Scawton Bridge) is approximately the road described as Sperragate in the Rievaulx Charter (179). The Charter goes on to say "from Sperragate, along it to the road which leads to the mill at Sproxton from Griff from the boundary of Sproxton to the High Road, where the cross is erected in the higher part of West Newton, from the ditch of Hescouwra to the ditch which overhangs the hosse of William de Walda". The cross is now gone, but it is thought to have been along Leysthorpe Lane, east of Oswaldkirk. The great road to the south is mentioned in a later charter from 1333: going towards Scawton and a bridge over the Rye, also "a Fee road outside the ditches, for themselves, (men of Sproxton) their carts and beasts carrying their goods between their grange of Griff and the sheep cote" (180).

THE SOUTHERN FRINGE

WELBURN - HAROME - SPROXTON AREA

The road from Fadmoor to Houeton (a lost village near Welburn) is mentioned in a charter of 1154 AD "the road called Meregate between the wood of Houeton (Howkeld) and the wood of Kirkebi and the wood of Fadmoor ---- and from the said Meregate to the great road"(probably Sperragate). Another road called Fragate led from Lund (SE 661860) to the road of Winbleton (Wombleton) in 1154. Stonycross near Wombleton road junction with A170 may be the Spelcros mentioned in 1145 AD (181).

Parker says "the road from Sproxton to Golden Square was made in 1758, previously it was a Pack & Saddle road" (134). Cooper (181) describes a road crossing the low ground by Sproxton Hall and Low Woods. There is little trace of it today. There was a ford east of Low Woods leading to Lock Yatt Lane and to the Harome-Helmsley road which the previous road might have used. In a field to the north the remains of brickworking can be found (SE 631829.)

Another old road passed east of Harome Heads to Highthorn, south of Beadlam. It is visible on air photos by A.L. Pacitto, at SE 649844 where it was a hollow-way before ploughing recently. Much stone came out of it and the rigg and furrow changed direction on reaching its course. Local folk though it was Roman.

Another road 10ft wide of small limestone cobbles was excavated at the east wing of Beadlam Roman Villa in 1973. Cooper says the road from Lock Yatt Lane went to a ford on Riccal Beck and went in the direction of Beadlam Grange up an old disused road crossed by the present A170 highway. He says it passed through the west side of Beadlam village to join the rigg road by Ellergate and Pockley Moor (p41). Old George Bumby who lived to be 100 years old favoured this route.

HELMSLEY - PICKERING - SCARBOROUGH

The limestone shelf under the southern lee of the North York Moors offered good drainage and thereby comparatively dry travelling along a good east-west route. It has been followed since Saxon times; note the string of place names ending in 'ton'.

From Beadlam going east the old route was by Nawton and Kirkdale and its ford, where it was crossed by the Meregate, thence through Kirkbymoorside, through West End and the market place (Piercy End was not a main thoroughfare until later), the Old Road by Howe End and down to Kirby Mills and Keldholme. It continued over the common to Catter Bridge - mentioned as 'Chatwatt' in a charter of King John in 1201 (182). The same charter names a lime kiln next to the River Dove and the ditch of Keldholme Priory land.

The modern A170 follows bypasses avoiding Kirkdale and Kirkbymoorside built in the early part of the 20th century and 1940 respectively - the latter to help the military in the event of a German invasion.

At Sinnington the river Seven would have to be forded or bridged before climbing onto the higher ground of Wrelton Cliff. In Sinnington there was a Saxon Church, a medieval chapel and also a hall of the Latimers; so much traffic in those days. Sinnington bypass was built 1931-33. From Sinnington the track could have followed the footpath from the Hall and Church by Coppice to Wrelton crossing the Roman road on the way to Wrelton. To Pickering it would have used the present line through a succession of old villages on the edge of the dip-slope.

At Pickering it was joined at Keld Head by the road from Marton called 'Street Lane' which may have branched from the Roman road below Wrelton. There was the medieval chapel of St. Nicholas at Keld Head (183) where air photos show possibly earlier sites. Marshall in 1790 says "all roads in Pickering district were flat and muddy or hollow-ways - now the public roads at least are usually barrel shaped and the banks of the hollows thrown down."

At Thornton Dale Jeffrey mentions "an ancient flagged causeway up Applegarth to Roxby Castle, or a packhorse track at a more easy gradient than the present Pickering Road, but tradition has it that it was laid for milk-maids to go to milk cows in the Aunums" (184). Roxby Castle (SE 828830) was a manor of the Hastings family, later enlarged by Sir Richard Cholmley who "led many wain (wagon) loads of stones from Pickering Castle to re-build Roxby in the mid 16th century". It is likely the causeway dates from that time or later.

From Thornton Dale a well used road went north-east by Outgang to Nabgate (SE 863845) and Stonygate Moor north of Allerston. The track may take its name from this moor, running the length of Sand Dale by tumuli towards the west end of the Red Dike. Here it turned north-east to join the track to Robin Hood's Bay skirting the end of Troutsdale. Branches went down Adderstone Rigg (Roman finds, also at Stoneclose Rigg). Most of this area has been obliterated by the forestry plantations. See Sewell (185).

East from Thornton Dale the line of the A170 follows an old road through Wilton where there are earthworks of the hall, later a castle, of Sir John de Heslerton. Ebberston had three manors, three granges and three mills. Thomas Westhorpe in 1336 had the Malton Grange (now Malton Cote) and a large stock of cattle and sheep, so the roads to Scarborough and Malton must have been well used. Brompton had a castle for a period and Ayton a pele-tower later enlarged as a castle of the de Ayton and Eure families and, later, less prominent families. The present tower is of 15th century date and was ruinous by the end of the 17th century (186).

From Ayton it is only three miles to Scarborough and five miles to Filey. From the sea ports much fish was carried inland. Once a year after 1248, the Abbot of Whitby had to send to the master of St. Leonard's Hospital, York 1500 red and 1500 white herrings, handed over at the cross-roads in Thornton Dale. Jeffrey says "many a yokel would watch with interest the Hospitallers taking over this huge load" (187).

LOCKTON - LEVISHAM

Two roads mentioned in medieval charters run north and north-west from Levisham, named Limpsey Gate Lane and Braygate Lane. In a grant, Ralph Bolebec (183) gave 52 acres of land between the arable land and the fosse towards the north and between the roads extending towards the moor, in a place called Dundale and 29 acres on the west of the west road 'Braygate' and the east road 'Limseygate'. Limpsey gate went on northwards over Levisham Moor turning north-east to Saltergate Bank Top where it is cut by a Cross-Ridge Dike - Gallows Dike, a double ditched bank, still forming a boundary line set with stones. Another east-west route, Scampston Way from Pifelhead Wood, Newtondale joins Saltergate Bank just below the escarpment and probably continues as Old Wife's Way to the south-east (p31).

ROSEDALE - SPAUNTON - NORMANBY

It was not until the Norman revival of the monasteries that connections between the Priory at Rosedale and the monastic church at Lastingham are recorded; by then Spaunton Grange and Manor became important (189). Old tracks leave the Beggars' Track (p12) west of the three howes, over Spindle Thorn to veer towards Lastingham and Spaunton on the Knowl at SE 717915. South from the 650ft knowl, they merge into 30-40 hollow-ways on the slope to the south towards High Cross (now vanished), which stood where these tracks were crossed by the Hutton-Lastingham road at Spaunton Bank Foot. Spaunton Bank Foot was never a hamlet until miners' cottages were built in the mid 19th century. Just east is Mary Magdalen's Well, one of the Holy Wells of Lastingham. It is a tiny spring but before a small runlet was made it supplied water to Lastingham Mill. In the 1950s it was almost lost in vegetation and rushes but was excavated by Harold Frank who found a crude trough which was entirely hidden and carved a stone giving the name of the well, as people had difficulty in locating it. During his excavations he found some pottery. Two 12th-13th century jug rims, a few body sherds and one body sherd of a calcite-gritted jar, possibly Roman or Anglian, give some indication of the long use of the well.

Hollow-ways on the east side of Spaunton Bank remain though the road is modern. Spaunton is one of the oldest settlements in Ryedale. It has produced evidence from the Neolithic to post medieval periods and had the Manor (mentioned above), also a windmill in medieval times, east of Lidsty Hill. The road from Lastingham to Appleton has a High Cross at SE 734887 where a lane leads to Wensdale Lane in the vicinity of the lost villa of Baschebi (190).

The Appleton Low Cross at the junction of Hamley Lane is a curious structure - a large flat slab with a hole in the side and traces of a recess for a plate. One local thought it was formerly the stocks. Both crosses are mentioned in medieval charters and other documents between 1160 and 1500. St. Mary's Abbey had a grange here and there was an elusive chapel in the Holm (191). To the south and west many limestone quarries were dug until the present century. Hargreaves ran a large limestone crusher and quarry on the edge of the common.

From Spaunton another old road, now lost, followed the lane south towards Lingmoor and passed the site of a Roman aisled house excavated by A.H. Whitaker in 1964-5 (192). This was a 3rd-4th century farm and several querns for grinding corn were found, with evidence of weaving in loom-weights and spindle-whorls. On the Appleton side of the lane a late Roman cist burial was found in 1900 (now in the Yorkshire Museum) and in the village a coin of Gordianus III (AD 238-44.)

South and west of Appleton le Moors near Ings Barn at the top of the open common, the track from Spaunton Lane coming from Ings Balk joins the modern road. The Ings Balk (photo) is a remarkable raised bank 14ft wide and 6-8ft high. It was used as a field road for carts but was lowered in 1967. Its name suggests a boundary bank. The field is perfectly dry so there was no need to raise the road to avoid mud but the raised portion is about 220 yards long. From it tracks ran across the common through a small embanked enclosure, now ploughed down though still visible on air photos (193) which was possibly a Romano-British farmstead. Pottery of this period was found nearby.

A large tumulus stands at SE 725861 south of Appleton Common. It was excavated in 1947-8 by members of Leeds University Anthropological Society, but had been dug previously; only one small cremation and a Roman grey-ware base were found in it. It was 100ft in diameter and 8ft high with a massive kerb of stones 79ft in diameter. Another of the group remains close to the A170 and an example 75ft in diameter remains south-east of Sinnington Manor (SE 727857). Others of the group have been ploughed down. Many finds of flint implements and stone axes come from the vicinity.

The present A170 is crossed here near Catter Bridge (p54). On a 225ft hill of boulder clay south-west of Sinnington Manor a small paved area was excavated in 1962. It is the floor of a Romano-British hut which produced pottery of the 4th century AD and pieces of broken quern-stones (194). The owner, Capt. James Holt, could not understand why the Britons should have farmed on this hard sticky clay. It is likely the hill was tree covered 1700 years ago and the soil less sticky. A slight hollow track can be seen winding up from the south.

The lane below between Catter Bridge and Little Edstone is called Lime Road. Lime was led down to the Vale of Pickering from numerous quarries around the southern slope of the Corallian Limestone hills. Keldholme Priory owned one in the mid 12th century. They were still in use with their kilns until the mid 20th century when the industry moved to other districts and lime was not in demand.

Normanby is on a good route via Marton and Great Barugh to Malton. At Normanby Hill (SE 732822) there was a large double-diked enclosure mentioned in the Honour of Pickering as belonging to the Abbot of St. Mary's York. He had a grange there and a hoard of coins and a silver ingot of 1200-1250 AD was found on the hill (195). Medieval potsherds were found at a ford near the church. The hill was first enclosed in the time of Edward I according to the Jury of the Forest of Pickering in 1335. The low lying land, only 80ft OD, was liable to flooding. Whether the present Barugh Lane was used in the Middle Ages is doubtful. The Roman road passed only a mile eastwards, and if still usable would be the alternative (73).

There was a medieval manor at Great Barugh on top of the hill and its enclosure was often thought to be Roman, but no excavation has taken place there, though quernstones of the beehive type have been found at Barugh and Normanby. The present Newsham Bridge (SE 748761) only dates back to the 18th century, but no doubt wooden ones preceded it. This is the major river crossing in this part of the Vale, and would need a bridge, though there was a ford near Newsham Manor. After low swampy ground south of the bridge Amotherby would be at or near the crossing of the Malton-Hovingham Roman road and the Braygate Street on the Howardian ridge with Malton (p51) only three miles to the east.

BRIDGES

We have only limited information on bridges, from the Rievaulx Charters and Quarter Session records. I am indebted to John McDonnell for his help with this chapter.

On the single flag trods or footpaths the streams were crossed by "Brigsteean", narrow slabs usually some 6-8ft long by 3ft wide. Examples exist at the crossing of Whiteley Beck, west of Commondale (NZ 653107), north of Helmsley across Bogmire Gill near Hazel Green at SE 608917 - a single slab. At NZ 902061, east of Sneaton Thorpe is a slab 9ft long, 2ft wide, 3-4ins thick, only 3ft above the water. This has wooden rails on the sides. Further east are two smaller slab bridges - slab 4 x 2ft and 4-5ins thick. Many of these slabs were displaced or broken and wooden foot bridges took their place. Some crossings had stone culverts, a form still used in the mid 19th century, as on the Rosedale Mineral railway at Rosedale Head and Reeking Gill.

Religious communities seem to have been responsible for repairing bridges in the middle ages. In 1334 the Forest Eyre (for the Forest Court on behalf of the king) requested the Prior and Hospital of St. John to repair the bridge and road of Pul near Foulbridge, (SE 913794, east of Yedingham) in 1334, which was common highway for carriages, carts, drifts, and pack-saddles (196). The Prioress of Yedingham was responsible for the road and bridge near her Priory, further west at SE 893797. In 1334 it was reported to be in good repair.

An early medieval reference to bridge building (or repairing) comes from Young (197). Reinfrid, Prior of Whitby Abbey, was performing a journey on the business of the monastery, and came to Ormesbridge where workmen were making a bridge over the Derwent, and leaping from his horse to assist them, without being on his guard, a beam fell upon him, and his skull was fractured and he immediately expired. He was buried at Hackness. The location of Ormesbridge is not known but it might have been at Hackness or at the bottom of Forge Valley.

Rievaulx. The late John Weatherill built up a description of the stone bridge that preceded the present one downstream from the abbey, which had been washed down in the great Rye flood of October 1754, from fragments found in the river bed. The stone was calcareous grit as was the choir of the Abbey. It had a wide pointed arch on the east side and a narrow one on the west side and the width including road and parapet, would be about 14ft.

Helmsley Rye Bridge is known to have had a medieval predecessor because there was a chapel on the approach to it (198).

A useful book on *Ancient Bridges in the North of England,* by E. Jervoise (199) calls Helmsley Bridge, medieval but the date in 'Helmsley' (198) is 1667. Nunnington Bridge (SE 670669) is dated by Jervoise as late 18th century, replacing one of 1671.

Newsham Bridge (SE 748761) was in existence in 1582 when part of £52 was granted for repairs mentioned several times between 1600 and 1900. It was rebuilt with stone from Appleton le Street 1754 and widened in 1908. It is still very narrow and twisting. Three arches are visible: originally it had four arches but the fourth may be still there, but buried? Somewhere here the Rye was bridged in Roman times, probably by a wooden structure on piles (200). I was told it spanned the mill race, unless they used the ford near the Manor which would be doubtful as it would have been impassible in time of flood.

Normanby Bridge (SE 735815) was mentioned by Leyland in the 15th century, but the bridge he saw has long since gone. He also saw a stone bridge with five arches at Pickering. Three are modern says Jervoise, but the fourth, a land arch, is evidently part of the bridge seen by Leyland.

Howe Bridge between Pickering and Malton (SE 809761) crosses the Rye three miles north of Malton. Called Ponte le Hou in the Malton Cartulary 1157- 89. Repaired by Rievaulx 1335. It was repaired at least twice in the late 16th century and possibly several times previously, between 1601 and 1695; there are fifteen recorded repairs and at least ten up to 1774. In 1888 £165 was spent on it but in 1938-40 it was rebuilt on a diversion at a cost of £15,600 and the old bridge and flood arches completely demolished.

Askew Bridge over the Seven between Lastingham and Cropton was important and in 1656 the inhabitants of Lastingham were charged with repairing 'the horse bridge over the Seven'. In 1681 the sum of £30 was allowed for its repair, 'it being of extraordinary great use to the country'.

Keldholme had only a ford up to the middle of the 17th century. A horse bridge was built in 1646 but was driven away and rebuilt in 1671 and 1712 (SE 718863).

Sinnington Bridge (SE 744858) is probably 18th century, but there are the remains of a curious little pack-horse bridge on the green near the old school. (Plate 18). It was investigated by the members of the Helmsley Archaeological Society in 1965 (201). It may have been over the tail race of a mill leat. There is a reference to one at the upstream end of the village, in a document of about 1180 when the local Roger de Clere granted the monks of St. Mary's Abbey, York, who owned the manor of Spaunton, and much other local property, a right of way for their wains and packhorses "from the ford on the road from Appleton to Sinnington down the valley to another ford near my mill, and so by the river bank, through the middle of the town of Sinnington". A road from Appleton le Moors ran south from the manor house over Dogcroft Hill by Holm Lane to a ford at SE 740868, where there are traces of stonework in the south-east bank. Further west is another ford called Sun Seven with hollow-ways on either side.

Tilehouse near Welburn (SE 680850). No longer on the A170 after recent alterations when the former line was taken further north and a new bridge made over Hodge Beck. The bridge of 1773 was widened at a cost of £140. There was a bridge probably of wood in 1594 as the Quarter Sessions at Malton granted £10 towards it. It was repaired four times between 1599 and 1659 and in 1668 Thirsk Magistrates granted £80 for rebuilding, probably in stone. Other repairs were in 1674 to 1742 when it was 'put on the county'. In 1742 the parapets were thrown down by a flood. In 1754 and in 1758 sixty four payments were made for repairs. In 1768 the Quarter Sessions at Thirsk contracted Robert Short (Jun) to rebuild at a cost of £160. It was rebuilt again in 1773. According to T. Parker (134) his great grandfather John Boyes of Wombleton brought freestone from the moors with four oxen and a horse in twenty loads, from March 2, 1769 to May 6, total cost was £26. 6s. 9d. He says the bridge took its name from a tile manufactory, formerly on the nearby hill west of the bridge. When the road was widened in 1960 many broken tiles were seen close by.

Various of the Eskdale bridges have already been mentioned in the text: Hunter's Sty at Westerdale (p17).

Dibble Bridge is west of Castleton (NZ 676078). It is very similar to Staithes Bridge (about 1720). An earlier form of the name is Depilbridge and it was mentioned in 1301 and 1539. The name may denote a bridge over a deep pool.

Bow Bridge at Castleton. The original bridge was called Eskethwayte and was standing in 1245. Probably rebuilt in stone about 1385, by the de Thewings. It had a high ribbed arch. When the railway came to Eskdale and a new bridge built on a diversion in 1873, the old one was sold to a builder for £5. At Castleton Canon Atkinson has a sketch of the earlier Bow Bridge, built in 1175-85 but destroyed in 1873 (202).

Duck Bridge, Danby (NZ 720077), was formerly known as Danby Castle Bridge. On the parapet is a stone bearing the arms of the Latimer and de Roos families. It may have been built before 1385. The name of the bridge was changed after it had been repaired by Mr. George Duck, of Danby, early in the 18th century. The Quarter Sessions, in October 1717 recorded a payment of £10. 7s. 6d., as a gratuity to help towards the cost of repairs. Jervoise thinks it probable the bridge must have been practically rebuilt at that time. The total span is 14 yards and the width between the parapets 6 feet 6 inches. This bridge has paved trods approaching it on two sides. Like Beggar's Bridge it survived the great floods of 1930-31. (Plate 19).

The Lealholm Bridge is mentioned in the North Riding Bridge Book of 1888. "(the bridge) at the village of Lealholm was only 7ft 10ins wide but has been widened to 15ft 6ins and is now become a great carriage road." It is mentioned in the Quarter Session records in 1584 to 1674.

Beggar's Bridge at Glaisdale is described on page 21.

Egton Bridge, (NZ 804052) p39, was said to be 'in great decay', in 1618 when the North Riding allowed £60 for its repair. It was called a 'foot and horse bridge' in 1619 and was for their use only. Previously it was in great decay. More repairs took place in 1635 and 1663 and on many other occasions up to 1930. It was destroyed in the flood of July 23rd 1930, and replaced by a metal structure, still used.

Grosmont Bridge. Three arched, mentioned in 1580, newly built in 1615 and in 1631 rebuilding. Many grants for repairs up to 1917. Another possible site of a Roman bridge (203).

Sleights Bridge. According to the Whitby Chartulary, it would appear this bridge was built by Peter Abbot of Whitby by permission of Reginald de Rosallas, owner of the land. It was built of stone. In the Guisborough Chartulary it was called Briggwath, the district still has that name. It was possibly a low foot or horse bridge with a ford alongside. There appears no record of it until 1711 when £100 was granted for repairs. There were more repairs in 1725 when it was 'driven down by violent flood'. John Baines was instructed to build a bridge for not more than £200, but in 1727 the Quarter Sessions at Northallerton received a report that the work was careless. It began to sink and the contractor lost his life. In 1755- 62 Robert Short (Jun) was to rebuild it for £550 and they paid a man to keep a ferry going during rebuilding. There were many more payments at the Quarter Sessions to 1880. It was destroyed by the severe flood in July 1930 and replaced by a cantilever bridge at a higher level in 1931. A new road replaced the old one by the Esk which was subject to flooding.

Whitby Bridge. No doubt there was a bridge here from very early days for the needs of the Abbey, though records point to the early bridges here in line with Baxtergate. Even earlier there may have been a ford at Boghall at the bottom of Waterstead Lane, traces of a log causeway or ford have been found here. The early bridges were of timber, probably from Collier Ghaut across to Virgin Pump Ghaut. There were shops on the 16th century bridge, mentioned in a will of 1541. (Test Ebor). In 1628 it was expected to have a draw-bridge. Young has a sketch (204). Grants of pontage were made in 1351 and 1361. The bridge was rebuilt in timber costing £110 in 1571. In 1641 Quarter Sessions at Thirsk had a complaint that a ship had forcibly entered the draw-bridge and thrown the scaffolding into the sea. There are many records for the damage from ships and repairs from 1642 to 1826.

It was rebuilt in stone at a cost of £3,000 in 1766 and since has been replaced at least twice. It was rebuilt on new site in 1834-5 for £2,600, as a swing bridge. Between 1849 and 1866 there were very heavy expenditures - about £175 per annum, including a new engine, new decking and wages of operators. In 1906 it was transferred to Whitby UDC and in 1909 rebuilt as an electric swing bridge for £4042. In 1936 the North Riding County Council granted £426 towards reconstruction. It was not until 1980 that a second bridge was built at Whitby, half a mile upstream between the high ground at Airy Hill and Larpool Lane. It was opened by the Marquis of Normanby on 21 March 1980.

Foul Bridge (SE 914795) one mile east of Yedingham Bridge was built in 1075. No longer in existence it was close to Templar's House, remains of which can be seen incorporated into the present farm house. (224)

Further information on bridges can be found in Jervoise (199), The Rievaulx Chartulary (133) and 'Helmsley' (198).

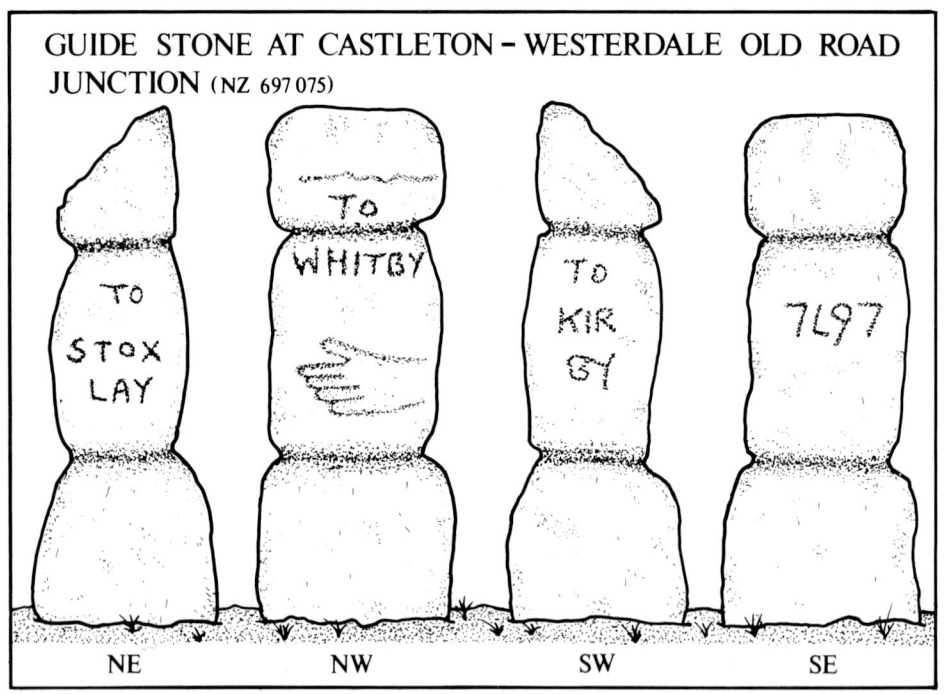

FIG. 1

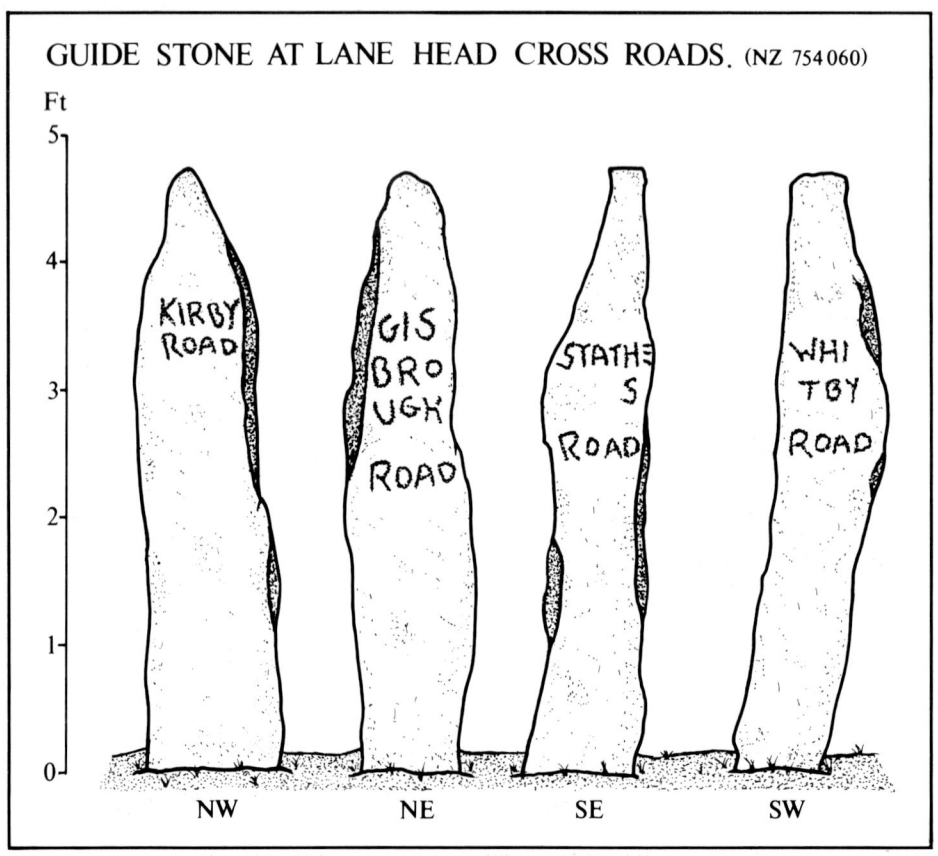

FIG. 2

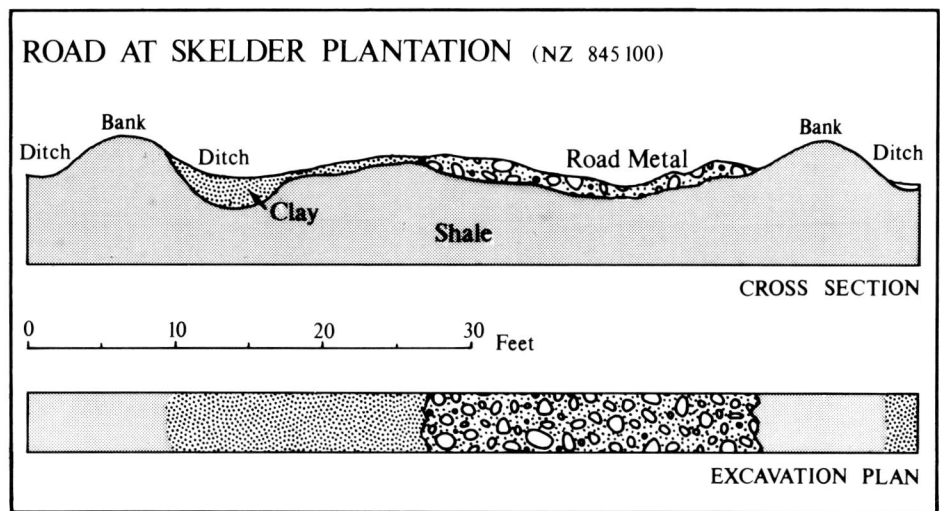

FIG. 3

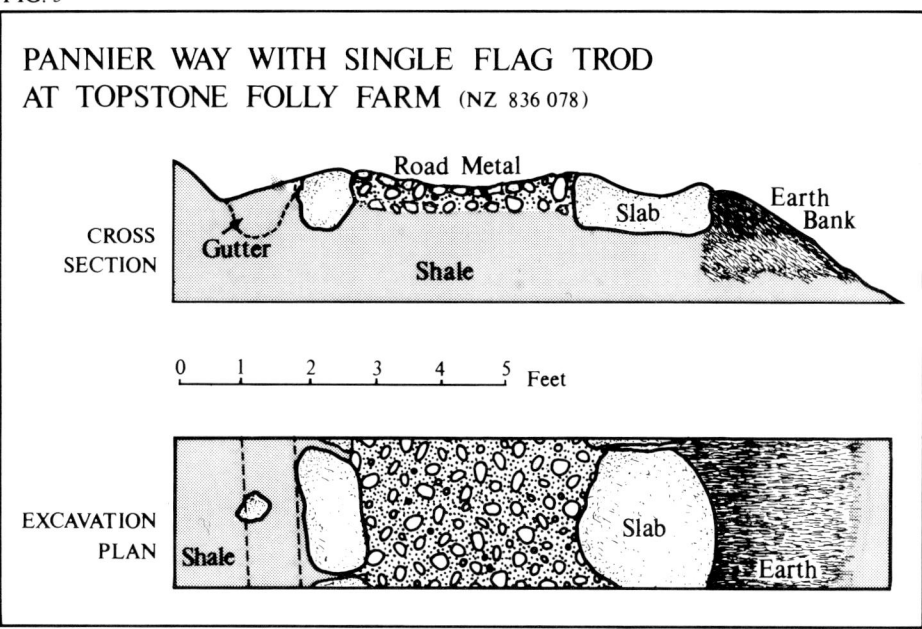

FIG. 4

FIG. 5

Guide Stone North of Hutton-le-Hole (693926)
Standing by the old hollow-way this early sign post is close to the present road.

Roadmen's Stone (676012)
This stone marks the north end of a roadman's 'stint' above Farndale.

Ralph Cross
A prominent moorland cross adopted as the National Park Emblem in 1974. Photo 1982.

Plate 3

Hunter's Sty - Westerdale
Extensively restored in 1878. Photo c. 1963.

Lane Head Stone Busco Beck, Lealholm (754060)

Plate 5

Beggar's Bridge - Glaisdale
A fine pack horse bridge over the River Esk c. 1619.

Paved Causeway over Lealholm Moor
A typical paved way across open moorland. This section was uncovered in 1986.

Monk's Walk - Sneaton
A well preserved trod in Cock Mill Wood photographed in the 1960s.

Plate 8

Malo Cross
A boundary marker at the foot of Whinney Nab near Saltergate.

Roman Road - Goathland
One of the best preserved Roman roads in Britain photo: NYCL Unne Collection c. 1960.

The Old Salt Road
*An ancient hollow-way over Snod Hill photographed in 1937.
Now inside the boundary of RAF Fylingdales.*

Thurkilsti on Skiplam Moor c. 1955
*One of several important medieval trackways over the moors.
This section has now been ploughed down.*

Lilla Cross on Sil Howe
*Dating from the 7th century, Lilla Cross was moved from its original position to Sil Howe in 1952.
It was restored to Lilla Howe in 1962.*

Waymarker above Bransdale (613952) photo c. 1955

Plate 13

Hand Stone on Urra Moor (597015)

Jennie Bradley Boundary Stone (611022)
The Feversham boundary stone of 1888 stands alongside the older cross in its stone socket.

Guide Stone on Rudland Rigg (654949)

Plate 16

The Cammon Stone on Rudland Rigg (626000)

Plate 17

Pack Horse Bridge - Sinnington
This curious structure may have bridged a mill leat.

Plate 18

Duck Bridge - Danby
Built c. 1385 and formerly known as Danby Castle Bridge.

An Early Packhorse Train

Plate 20

Appendix A

TYPES OF EARLY ROADS

1. STRATA REGALIS OR REGALIS VIA.
    - Royal Road - King's Highway
2. MAGNA VIA. Great Road
3. VIA COMMUNA. Public Road or Village Street.
4. PANNIER TRODS. Paved or Unpaved.
5. FOOTPATHS. Often paved alongside old roads.

The Latin names are used in medieval charters. Later 'gate' was the usual name, also street, as in the towns - York and Malton. There were bridges in Roman times though none have survived in Ryedale. Hints of Saxon or Norse bridges - Ormsbridge and Waltheof'(s) Bridge. There were ten bridges on the Derwent and at least five on the Esk. Chapels were placed on or near bridges - St. Ninian's at Whitby and St. Nicholas' Hospital at the end of Malton/Norton Bridge.

Appendix B

EXTRACTS FROM MEDIEVAL CHARTERS RELATING TO ROADS

There are several references to medieval roads in the Ryedale Charters. Atkinson has an article on translations of them (126). Others have been arranged, but not published, by Mr B Harrison.

Atkinson quotes an agreement dated 1170 between Abbot Aelred of Rievaulx and Abbot Roger of Old Byland (133). Byland grants to Rievaulx that they may have the "pontem laqueatum" (bridge) and retain their "ligna" (timber) brought together by the river Rye. The bridge is to remain the same height or if they wish to raise it they may raise it to the level of the banks. Most likely this was a wooden bridge. They also grant a road from the bridge through the wood to the field of Beghland (Byland), as far as the land extends towards Hestelsceit (Hesketh Grange), 18ft broad, and to mend the same road when there is need. This is one of the few records of making a road and building a bridge.

In the same charter p 179, it states "the boundaries between the brothers of Lauescales (Laskill) and the brothers of Snigleswath (Snilesworth), shall be the road which leads from Halmbi (Hawnby) to Cliveland -----".

In the Egerton Papers in the British Library is mentioned (205):

Boundaries of Whorlton & Snilesworth "as the water falls from Neleshou on both sides of Harthou, and then as the water divides to Pundcalehou, and as it falls to the Red Road (Rubera via)" - cf-Roppa which has the same meaning 'Red Road', possibly from red shale or ironstone water. The howes mentioned could be in the vicinity of Prod Howe, which is on the boundary at SE 529893, or Pin Howe just north of the boundary.

Appendix C

VEHICLES USED ON MEDIEVAL ROADS

The majority of travellers on these roads and pannierways either went on foot or horse-back. A good horse could go 40-50 miles a day in reasonable conditions. Wheeled vehicles were not much used for passengers. Chariots or whirlicotes were used only for Royalty or noblemen, and they must have been unbearably bone-shaking with their metal springs.

Mr. T.W. Parratt, in his very useful paper on *Northern Roads in the Middle Ages* (206) mentions information on the King's carter, William of London at Pickering in 1325-6 from the North Riding Records. William had a cart and six horses. His pay was 4½d per day - which included an assistants wages. The term used for this cart is defined as a Carecta and he is described as a Carectarius. At Rievaulx Abbey when Stephen de Meinill granted the Abbey a right of way to Greenhow, 'Hominibus et Carrettis Suis' is probably the same vehicle.

In the building of York Minster the Carecta carried lead, stone and lime. Two troughs and one lintel required three such carts. The medieval carts were also used for transporting corn, hay and timber. At Ampleforth in 1295 the bondmen had to carry nine Bigate of wood for fuel and the lord would find one Carecta and two Plaustra to cart hay. Parratt could not find the difference between a Carecta and a Biga. The Quadriga was probably drawn by a team of four and later became a wagon. In the 12th century a grant of a free right of way was given to St. Mary's Abbey, York, between Appleton and Sinnington, for pack animals and Quadrigae. Parratt refers to at least two dozen Medieval Latin names being known for different types of vehicles, including all those mentioned here, with none of them being described fully enough for the differences to be clear (206).

Canon Atkinson wrote that "the veritable wain, now never seen, was a narrow, long bodied vehicle with two wheels only at the hinder end. The front trailed along the ground except when lifted by the tractive power employed". This was very similar to the 'slide car' used in Wales and illustrated by Sir Cyril Fox in Parratt's article. Parratt thinks sleds developed into wains by the addition of wheels (206). Wains were usually drawn by oxen. Rievaulx had lent one to Lord Roos of Helmsley. Sleds were used on the moors and in Ryedale for many generations and survived until 1950 or later. The hard winter of 1947 saw many in use. Fittings for wayns are mentioned at Whitby Abbey in the 13th century. Waingate is the term used for several old roads. Marshall writing at Pickering in 1790 says "Fifty years ago, they (wains) were common - now not one left" (207).

For more information on vehicles see the Introduction.

Appendix D
GOODS AND MERCHANDISE CARRIED

IRON STONE & IRON BLOOMS. There were over 150 iron smelting (bloomery) sites in Cleveland and Eskdale, mainly 12th to 17th centuries. The products were taken by cart, sled or pannier pack. The Rosedale iron smith in 1348 had to deliver 16-18 stones of iron weekly to Spaunton (208).

GLASS was blown in Rosedale and at Hutton in the period 1570-1610 AD. This was most likely taken in pannier baskets.

TEXTILE industries flourished in the dales in the same period and the fulling and weaving process necessitated the transport of wool, cotton, kerseys and broadcloths. Linen was also woven.

TIMBER for house building and for the Whitby shipyards was carried from the Forest of Pickering, especially from Allan Tofts, Goathland.

SALT & FISH were carried from very early times from Whitby and Scarborough, Robin Hood's Bay and Coatham Marshes where Rievaulx monks had salt pans in the 13-15th centuries.

LIME. One of the earliest kilns mentioned was in 1201: the lime-kiln near Keldholme Priory next to the Duva (Dove), most likely near the quarry in Ravenswyke Park west of the road to Hutton le Hole. Lime was taken in large quantities from the southern slopes of the Corallian limestone hills north of the Vale of Pickering from the 18th century onwards. As many as 40-50 wagon loads could be seen halting at the moorland inns at Blakey, Hamer, Limekiln House, Chequers, Saltergate and Hope Inn. Moor coal was brought from Cleveland to the lime kilns and this made a profitable return trade in the 17-19th centuries - Sewell says John Atkinson of Castle House, Danby, brought in one season, 1830, and on consecutive days, forty wagon loads of lime, one and a quarter tons in each, from Hutton le Hole to Castleton. Working three wagons per day he drove an empty one in the early morning to the moor coal pits at Rosedale Head, left it there taking one he had left the previous day, now full of coal to Hutton where it was left to be emptied and filled with lime for the morrow, taking another wagon full of lime back to Danby (209).

The road from Hartoft via Hamer House was used for transporting lime. Joe Ford refers to it (23) and in 1868 George Cornforth took 20 loads of lime from Copton via Hamer. On the junction of the Hancow-Hartoft road at SE 753934, are the remains of John Harland's lime kiln of 1735, marked 'old kiln' on the old 6ins maps, but not on the modern 2ins series. Lime was taken from the Spaunton Lane and Lingmoor kilns over Appleton Common to Marton and Normanby. The route was called the 'Ord Lime road' in the late 19th century and is still named 'Lime Road' on the modern 2ins map. Kilns at Gibson's quarry in Cropton lane were in use until about 1950.

TILES made near Cropton and bricks from the Vale of Pickering were also transported at this period.

ALUM is discussed in detail in Appendix E.

Other items would be hay, corn (oats and barley), malt and manure (seaweed from the coast).

FAIRS AND MARKETS. There were many regular fairs and markets in North East Yorkshire, at which much trading was done. These would have attracted much traffic. See refs 210 & 211 for further information in articles by B. Waites and J.H. Rushton on fairs and markets in the area.

Appendix E
ALUM

This was a local industry from the early 17th until the mid 18th centuries. Pack horses and wagons were used and some mines had rail tracks.

Alum was used for fulling, dyeing and tanning. The process began in Greek and Roman times but appears to have been lost until the 16th century when Italian alum working employed 800 men. The monopoly was held by the Pope who forbade Christians to buy it from any other source.

Tradition credits Sir Thomas Chaloner of Guisborough with the discovery of Yorkshire alum. He noticed the rock and vegetation of the Italian sites were similar to that near Guisborough. He smuggled papal workmen to England (one story says in barrels) and after several trials succeeded in extracting alum. The Pope put a potent curse on him, but by 1609-12 there were four mines at Slapewath, Belman Bank, and West Bank (all near Guisborough) and also at Sandsend, employing hundreds of workmen. Other early mines were at Grosmont, Goathland, Eskdaleside, Stoup Brow (1752- 1817) Saltwick Nab, and Mulgrave Woods.

Coal had to be brought from Durham or West Yorkshire at great expense and the mines suffered from corrosion and the action of the sea on the cliffs.

Alum is a double salt, a combination of aluminium sulphate with either potassium sulphate or ammonium sulphate. Processing it was complicated, worked by rule of thumb methods. A layer of brushwood or gorse was piled on the ground. On this alum shale in lumps was placed to a height of two- three feet. This was lighted and caused the bituminous shale to burn. Further shale was added to a considerable height, and much care taken in keeping the internal temperature even. In windy weather the sides were plastered with slurry (burnt shale mixed with water), but if the fire was slow the interior of the heap was poked with rods. It seldom took less than a year to burn out one of the heaps, so several heaps were burning at the same time.

At Boulby and elsewhere, they managed to set fire by accident to jet shales which burnt for years.

When the burning process was ended the heap was allowed to cool slowly until it was 'mellow', then it was steeped in water in tanks or lead pans. The spent shale was thrown into the sea, and the 'liquor' concentrated to a specific gravity, determined according to tradition by floating an egg on it. The alum workers' secret was knowing the exact point at which to stop and to separate the impurities from the solution.

Two methods of manufacture were used locally. Potash alum was made from burning seaweed, centred on Staithes. Ammonium alum was produced by the substitution of urine for kelp. This was, like the former method, finally re-crystallised in wooden casks the staves of which could be loosened by knocking away the supporting hoops.

The peak of the alum industry came by the mid 18th century. In 1764 3200 tons at £22 per ton was recorded but a new process patented in Lancashire in 1860 put an end to the Cleveland industry. Loftus had finished by 1830, Eskdaleside and Peak had almost finished by 1860 and Sandsend about 1870. Remains can be seen at Boulby, excavated by Keith Chapman of Brotton, and at Kettleness. Sandsend's remains have almost gone.

Bibliography

(a) Useful lists of alum sites and also moor coal and iron pits can be found in the Notes compiled by J G Rutter under *Industrial Archaeology in North East Yorkshire* (212).

(b) Alum. Young's History of Whitby (213).

(c) A good account of alum working by Walter White (214).

(d) For Ironstone Chapman's *Gazetteer of Cleveland Ironstone Mines* (215).

(e) See also *Rosedale Mines and Railways* (17).

(f) For Medieval or earlier iron working, the author's *List of Early Iron - Working sites in N.E. Yorks*, and also in 'Helmsley' (216).
Also *Rosedale Medieval Iron Works* R.H. Hayes 1988

(g) For jet A useful paper by J.S. Owen (217).

(h) For medieval glass working see papers by Aberg and Crossley (119) and Hayes and Hemingway (120).

(i) Moor Coal. Helmsley p460 list by author only covers a few. See also paper by A.H. Whitaker (18) and Young's *History of Whitby* (218).

(j) Lime. See Young (218) and Moore R.F. (125). Very inadequate account - poor map & cover sketch of lime waggon incorrect.

Appendix F

PACK HORSES IN THE NORTH
BY S. EMILY LUMB

Reprint of original article in *North Country Lore and Legend*, Sept. 1890 (p397).

In the northern parts of Lancs and Yorks, pack-horses (galloways) were used as a means of conveying merchandise such as coal, wool, lime, malt, or corn, until about 1840, when the Lancs-Yorks railway was opened. A 'gang of galloways' consisted of 12-14 horses. They always walked in single file, the first horse wearing a collar of bells and known as the 'bell-horse'. They set off at 4 a.m. each horse with a pack on its back, secured there by a 'wanta' - a broad webbing belt, with ropes and hooks at both ends. First the webbing went round the horse for ease, then the ropes went over the pack, under the horse and fastened to the hooks. When light flagstones or slates were required to be carried, a 'hook-seam' was attached to the pack-saddle by means of a staple.

After starting the horses would generally be allowed to eat grass by the roadside or open spaces, as they went along; but the drivers when they considered they had had sufficient, would put on muzzles, which were like those of dogs, only a little more square. If the bell-horse, while grazing, happened to get behind the others, as soon as it was muzzled it knew the real travelling for the day had commenced, and would bore and push until its own honoured place as leader was gained. The bells it wore were seven, one ordinary shaped bells in the middle and three round ones on each side. These had a small slit in the bottom, through which a little molten metal had been passed to form a tongue. The bells were fixed to a leather collar, which was fastened to the top of the pack-saddle and hung loosely across the shoulders, so that they rang with every movement of the horse. Occasionally the men would walk ahead, a mile or so, in order to have a pint or a pipe at some well-known pub. The 'gals' understood this proceeding, and (if they were muzzled) would jog along as if their drivers were by their sides.

If the drivers were going on more than one day's journey, they would put up for the night at some wayside inn. First they would unfasten the 'wantas', throw down the packs in a sheltered yard, take off the muzzles and turn the horses into the 'croft' or 'paddock'. Next day they would be away again very early.

The roads they travelled were flagged in the middle with one broad stone, and were known as 'bridle styles'. I have heard them called 'Saddleroads' on account of the stones becoming so worn that they resembled a saddle. Also 'Roman roads' because the Romans laid a long line of stones for water to run down (probably from the line of bonding, or skid-dragstones thus worn, to be seen on the Roman road over Blackstone Edge, Halifax - Littleborough). Also called 'causey', pannier trods or 'streets'. Filling the packs and loading the 'gals' was very heavy work; consequently the farmers selected the strong men for drivers.

Their meals consisted chiefly of hung beef and fat bacon, fried together with thick oat-cakes and two quarts of home-brewed ale. While this was eaten the farmer's wife would make the 'waff' by mixing oatmeal, treacle and cream into the same pan after frying a little while it was rolled into balls, and eaten hot or cold.

The drivers generally dressed in knee-breeches, and calf-skin vests, and always carried a large stick. Their wives always listened for the tinkling of bells as a sign of their return home.

A friend, whose father kept pack-horses, has given me most information. His father's team generally carried malt, but sometimes took coals to the dale farms, where carts had difficulty in travelling. Such events were marked by a little festivity by the farmers - to have a 'gang' of coal was quite an event. In the sheep-clipping time, donkeys were also used as carriers, sometimes as many as forty packs of wool carried by them on one journey.

Appendix G

THOMAS HARWOOD

Thomas Harwood is mentioned in the text. He was a member of a family recorded in the dale as early as 1585. They were related to another old family, the Woodwarks of London House, Glaisdale Head. It is though he lived in a low stone house with mullioned windows, crucks and a salt box, opposite Hutton Lodge (NZ 745 033). A photograph of this house exists taken by William Hayes (father of author) about 1906. It had lost its thatch and had corrugated metal on the roof, but was still standing. The mullioned windows had gone but two small service or fire windows remained. A dated mark on a stone was

M
TH 1726

The M possibly stands for Maria Barry, his wife.

There are many stones inscribed by Harwood. A gatepost on the bank of Hardhill Gill has a long inscription of Francis Hartus 1737 carved by Harwood. The longest inscription by him is on a stone 200 yards south-east of Hardhill House, about a right of way for John Campion. Harwood also put his markers on the causeway made down New Lane from Lealholm to Glaisdale in 1769.

The erecting of waymarkers or guide stones took place after the Justices at Northallerton on October 2nd 1711 ordered Guide Posts to be erected throughout the North Riding, and all surveyors in every parish had to order posts to be erected at the crossways (219). This is a likely first date for the making of most of the paved trods.

There is an informative article on Harwood by Percy Burnett in the Whitby Naturalists Club report (220).

Appendix H
JOSEPH T. SEWELL: MEDIEVAL ROADS SOUTH AND WEST OF WHITBY

Several references to this pioneer work occur in the text. It was first published in 1922 by the Whitby Literary & Philosophical Society in their 100th annual report and reprinted in 1971 by Horne & Son of Whitby. There is a short account of J.T. Sewell in the 1971 edition.

Joseph Taylor Sewell J.P. was born at Malton in 1857. As a boy of 9 he moved with his family to Whitby where his parents were in partnership with a wholesale and retail grocer at St Ann's Staith. He was educated at Ackworth & Bootham (Quaker Schools). Ill health caused an early semi-retirement in 1915. He spent much time at 'The Cottage' Goathland Green, built by his father and aunt. His great friend was Louis Roland who was very active in archaeology and local history.

Like many of us "J.T.S." hoped to record all his findings - but he died in 1925 at the age of 68.

He collected much useful information on old roads and pannierways, several of which have now gone. Though somewhat disconnected and lacking a map, his account does give details of many routes now lost, or obliterated by the Forestry Commission. Whether they are all medieval is open to question, and it is unlikely much of the Roman road remained in use even in the 16th century. He did actually see a large drove of ponies and donkeys in Helmsley market place in 1868 and a similar arrival of coal at Castleton - he says he always looked back on this scene as depicting the type of traffic on the pannierways in ancient times (221).

Appendix J
'STY' ROADS

The suffix 'sty' recurs frequently in the area. It is thought to come from the old Danish for a 'ladder' hence a steep path although the modern English word 'stile' has a similar meaning and comes from The Old English 'stigel', meaning to climb. John McDonnell and I have compiled the following catalogue of references of examples in the area.

ARLOTESTYE Source NNRS (NS) I, 25. Allerston. Marking bounds of Allerston - Hazlehead Moor?

BORUSCHOWSTILE Source Yorks. Deeds (YAS) V, 45. Everley, par Hackness.

BRIDLE STYLES A term used by S.Emily Lumb in her article - 'Pack Horses in the North' Appendix 'F'

CATSTY Name of a pathway up Hutton West Wood, now disused. Also a pathway up the west side of Ousegill Beck, Bransdale.

CATTERSTY Name of a bank, wood and gill, in ravine and wood down to the coast N. of Skinningrove; shown on 1850 OS map, now followed by later roads. A Catter Bridge between Sinnington and Keldholme Chatwith, 14th century may be derived from 'Ket or Coed' Celtic for wood.

CRAGGISTYE NNRS (NS) I,25 Allerston - Marking Bounds of Allerston - Adderstone.

CUSTO-/CUSTE-/CUNTESTI Percy Chartulary 119,142. 'viam que venit ad Samare apud Hakeness, que vocatur Custody'. Mr Marriott (Scarborough) notes a Cuneysgate on 6" O.S. ref. 988877, on line between Seamer and Hackness.

ERNALDSTY Old road from Kildale to Hutton Low Cross. From Ernald or Arnald de Kildale, a branch of the Percy family.

GAYTSKI HEWIC BECK Beck near the Roman Road on Wheeldale Moor. Yorks Inquests. I.p 50. (Inq at Pickering 12519-2.) the late Job Todd of Hutton-le-Hole called this road 'the Skivic' in 1935.

GRUNSTY Name for track east of Cropton Mill 19th century.

HALLGATESTIE NNRS (NS) I,25. Bounds of Allerston - nr. Newgate Foot.

HASTY BANK O.S. map. N. end of Bilsdale.

HOLTHORPESTI Yorks Deeds (YAS) VII,131. Hovingham-Howthorpe.

HUNTERSTY Smith, Place names NR., 135. 'In Westerdale' (1301) (Notes: cf VCH(NR) II, 415 - 'Hanyiestrete' in Westerdale (1545). Another Huntersty in Bellerby (Swaledale) - Riev. Ch. 399 - 400.

KERBYSTIE Yorks Deeds (YAS) X,148-9. Scawton-Cold Kirby, on Saxton 1598 map.

KIDSTYE Farm in Newtondale (SE 830946).

KIRKESTY NNRS (NS) 11,183. Newton Rawcliff. Wood 'inter molendium de Neuton et Kirkesty'.

LANGESTY Yorks Deeds (YAS) X 107: Guisbro. Ch. I,172. Hutton Lowcross.

LIDSTY HILL Bank S of Lastingham to Appleton Lane.

MIDDLESTY Valley near Osmotherley sketch on p428 of Edmund Bogg's *VALE OF MOWBRAY*.

NUNNESTY Guisbro'Ch. II,225. Biggin Houses nr. Ugthorpe. Handale nuns?

OVERSTY/OVERSTYRIGGE Above in Forest of Pickering and north of Hackness. NNRS(NS) II,xxxv, 62. Forest of Pickering. Scene of deer poaching by aMeynill, a Mauley, et al.

POTTERSTY Guisbro' Ch. II, 250. Marske.

RISHESTY NRRS(NS) I,11. Woods in West Ward of Pickering Forest.

RUDSTYBANK NNRS(NS) I,210. Blansby Park, Pickering.

SHAKERSTYE As above. Near above.

SILFOUSTY Whitby Ch. II,448. Hackness area. Cf. Silpho (brow).

SWINESTICHAGE Whitby Ch. I,34. Hckness area. Cf. next entry.

SWINSTEY (STY) On the moor above Goathland, towards Egton-Randy Mere Road.
SWINESTYE Crag and Hill north of Osmotherley.
SWINE STYE HILL Rosedale (SE 709978).
SWYNSTIBECK Yorks Deeds (YAS) VIII,71. Guisbro' area. Cf. above.
THURKILSTI   (1)   Riev. Ch,. 16-20.
                  (2)   Yorks Deeds (YAS) I,123; Nawton area.
                  (3)   Early Yks. Ch. IX,231; bounds of Welburn. Cf.R.B.Turton, Cleveland Nat. Proceedings, 1932, pp.112-4.

Abbreviations

Ch	Charters
NRRS(NS)	North Riding Records (New Series)
VCH(NR)	Victoria County History (North Riding)
YAS	Yorkshire Archaeological Society.

Appendix K

HOW MUCH SMUGGLING WENT ON WE SHALL NEVER KNOW!

Pannier ways are often called 'Smugglers Ways'. Brandy Bridge, Gin Garth and Whisky Thorn are place names which all testify to traffic in spirits. Illicit stills are spoken of at various places. One was kept by an old woman at the lime quarries near Hutton in Douthwaitedale, Whisky Johnnie kept a still at his sawmill: Cellars under a house at Yoadwath (Old Horse Ford) were said to have been hiding places for kegs of brandy. Gin Garth in Westerdale was said to be the resort of smugglers and drinking parties from places as distant as Kirkbymoorside!

If you wake at midnight and hear a horse's feet,
Don't go drawing back the blind or looking in the street
Them that asks no questions isn't told a lie,
Watch the wall, my darling, while the Gentlemen go by.

Five and twenty ponies,
Trotting through the dark -
Brandy for the Parson,
Baccy for the Clerk;
Laces for a lady, letters for a spy,
And watch the wall, my darling, while the gentlemen go
  by!

(Rudyard Kipling)

Appendix L

PANNIERWAYS GUIDESTONES

Mention is made of several inscribed guide stones or waymarkers.

- p15. Stone on Westerdale Old road. Westerdale-Stoxlay-Kirby. Whitby.
- p16. Broken stone inscribed D-Danby and G-Guisborough.
- p19. ROSDAL WHITBY - George Gap Causeway.
- p19. Lane Head Stone. STATHES ROAD WHITBY KERBY road, and GUISBORO ROAD.
- p20. Elm Ledge. Fallen stone CASILTON-WHITBY-STOXLA IX.
- p23. Lady cross - GUIS---ROAD 1771 WHITBY. --AD.
- p38. COMMON LONING. L (1699).
- p41. N of Skiplam Nab - weathered guide stone - This way to STOKSLEY. This way to KIRBY. This way to GUISBRO. This way to BILSDALE.
- p42. TO STOXLA, THIS KIRBY ROAD. S--TH ?? HELMSLEY ROAD.
- p42. Waymarker - TO INGELBY AND STOXLEY. TO KIRBY AND HELMSLEY. TO GUISBORO. The Hand Stone is nearby. THIS WAY TO KIRBY (broken- crook hand. On N - THIS IS THE WAY TO STOXLA.
- p45. INGLEBY GREENHOWE. 1711 guide stone near vicarage.
- p46. RUDLAND RIGG. On track to FARNDALE - THIS KERBY ROAD. -- THIS PICKERING ROAD - STOXLY ROAD. WILLEY STOUP --- KIRBY RODE. COCKANS CROSS. STOXLA RODE. KIRBY RODE. FARNDALE ROAD & BRANSDALE RODE.
- p49. Stone near Kepwick on Hambleton Street CT 1770.

Many of the old stones have gone - some broken up to mend the road.
STOKESLEY is mentioned on 7 stones.
WHITBY on 5 stones.
KIRKBYMOORSIDE on 6 stones.
GUISBOROUGH on 5 stones & G on stones in Northdale.
STAITHES on 2; DANBY on 2; CASTLETON on 1; HELMSLEY 1;
 BLOWATH 1; WESTERDALE 1; BILSDALE 1; ROSEDALE 1;
INGLEBY 1; FARNDALE 1; BRANSDALE 1.

NOTES AND REFERENCES

Abbreviations

Breakell — *Stone Causeways of The North York Moors*, Footsteps Books, Hebden Bridge, 1982. Republished by North York Moors National Park Department, Helmsley, 1987 under the title *Old Pannier Tracks*.

Cruck Buildings — Hayes RH and Rutter JG. Some Cruck-Framed Buildings in Ryedale and Eskdale *SDAS Report No.8*, 1972.

EM — Elgee F., *Early Man in North-east Yorkshire* (Gloucester 1930)

Forty Years — Atkinson, JC *Forty Years in a Moorland Parish,* 1981, revised 1908 (page references throughout to 1908ed.) H & H Misses J. Horsman and A Haigh of Scarborough, Notes on Flagged Paths in Hawsker-with-Stainsacre area (unpublished June 1964), in possession of R. H. Hayes.

Helmsley — *A History of Helmsley, Rievaulx & District*, Helmsley Group of Yorkshire Archaeological Society, ed. McDonnell, J. (York 1963).

MOW — Atkinson, Rev. J.C., *Memorials of Old Whitby* (London 1894)

RFM — Ryedale Folk Museum, Hutton-le-Hole.

Sewell — Sewell, J.T., *An account of some medieval roads crossing the moors, south and south west of Whitby.* 2nd ed., Whitby 1971.

SDAS — Transactions of the Scarborough & District Archaeological Society, from 1958. In 1980 the Society changed its name to the Scarborough & District Archaeological and Historical Society. (Ed. Rimington, F.C).

Turton — Turton RB '*A few Cleveland Place-names*, in Proceedings of The Cld Naturalists' Field Club Vol. IV, Pt. 2, 1928-32.

VCH — *Victoria County History of Yorkshire* (North Riding). See note 33.

Wade's Causeway — Hayes RH and Rutter JG. Wade's Causeway. *SDAS Report No. 4,* 1964.

WNR — Whitby Naturalists Club Reports (1938-47)

Woodwark — Woodwark T.H., *The Crosses of the North York Moors,* 4th ed. (Whitby 1970).

YAJ — *Yorkshire Archaeological Journal* (Yorkshire Archaeological Society, Leeds).

Young — Young, Rev. G., *History of Whitby,* 2 vols., 1817. (reprinted Caedmon, Whitby, 1976).

1. Breakell, p10.
2. Breakell, p11.
3. Bryant, Sir A. *The Medieval Foundation*.
4. Sewell, p38. Quoting from North Riding Records, 1577/1588, of Queen Elizabeth.
5. Fiennes, Celia. Journeys, 1685 - 98. Editor C Morris, 1947 edition, p192.
6. Forty Years.
7. Quarter Sessions Record, 1889. p146-7
8. Sewell, p24
9. Information from D. Wood of Lodgefield Farm.
10. Heavysides, M. *Rambles in Cleveland,* published by author, Stockton-on-Tees, 1903.

11. Rushton J H, 'Keldholme Priory'. *Ryedale Historian* I pl5-23 (1965)
12. Dodsworth, R and Dugdale, W. *'Monasticum Anglicanum'*, Vol.5, p665.
13. Whale Jaws re-erected Ryedale Folk Museum "SHIP VALIANT" 1792 owned by the Shepherds of Douthwaite.
14. Honour of Pickering 1310 AD & 1334. *North Riding Records,* Vol 3 p49.
15. Pacitto A L, Rudland Close *Ryedale Historian No 2* p20-43, 1966.
16. Young p 675.
17. Hayes R H & Rutter J G, Rosedale Mines & Railway. *SDAS report No. 9* 1974, p8-9
18. Whitaker A M, 'Coal Mining in Bransdale & Farndale in the 18th Century' *Ryedale Historian No. 4*, 1969 (p55).
19. Sewell p24-25.
20. Elgee H W , 'An Early Bronze Age Burial in a boat-shaped Wooden Coffin from N.E. Yorks'. *Proceedings of The Prehistoric Society*, 1949.
21. Calendar of Patent Rolls, Edward III, 1345-48 Mentioned in Dugdale, Baronage of England. Vol. Ip 541.
22. Whitaker A H, 'A History of Farndale in the Later Middle Ages' *Ryedale Historian No. 2* p 57-58, 1966.
23. Joseph Ford, *Reminiscences of Danby*, 1944.
24. Hartley, M and Ingilby, *J Life in the Moorlands of North East Yorkshire*, Dent, London, 1972.
25. RAF air photos, No. 4450-4451.
26. Crosland, R.Wilfrid *Yorkshire Treasure*, 1948.
27. Atkinson J C, *Gentleman's Magazine*. 1893 p22.
28. Baker G. *Unhistoric Acts*. Records of our early Friends (Quaker) in N. E. Yorks, Bradley Bros, London, 1906.
29. Woodwark. Fat Betty is No. 14.
30. Dimbleby G. W. 'The Ancient Forest of Blackamore'. *Antiquity, Vol. 35, No. 138*, June 1961. pl23-9. Also by Dimbleby GW *'The development of British Heathlands and their soils'*, Oxford 1962, p43. Site VII, p63.
31. EM, p209.
32. EM, p139-40.
33. Forty Years p443.
34. Conn House. Elgee (EM p233) thought it a Gaelic name meaning corner or angle.
35. EM, p149
36. Hayes, RH The Chambered Cairn and Adjacent Monuments on Great Ayton Moor, N. E. Yorks. *SDAS Research Report No.7*, 1967, p35.
37. Sewell p29 comments on 'Quakers Path' from Baker, 'Unhistoric Acts' (ref 24).
38. Elgee, *Moorlands of NE Yorkshire*, 1912, p19.
39. Hunter's sty. Sti-stig Anglo-Saxon for hill road, sty still used for a ladder in local dialect. See Appendix J.
40. *Victoria County History of Yorkshire*, (N. Riding). 3 vols, 1914-23, ed. W. Page and others. Vol 3, p260.
41. Young, p756.
42. Helmsley p436-7. Rievaulx's most isolated grange NZ 657016 (R.H. Hayes).
43. This was simply a stone way-marker like that near the Cheese stones higher up Baysdale. Shinnera Cross was of the same type, though an earlier cross could have been replaced.
44. Hob Hole bloomery excavated by F A Aberg (unpublished).
45. Spratt, D; Hayes, RH; Close, RS. 'Romano - British Site at Crag Bank Wood, Kildale'. *Y.A.J. 47,* 1975, p61-68.
46. Close RS & Hayes R H, 'Pale End', *Y.A.J. p687-700, 1966.*

47. Close R.S. 'Hut sites on Percy Cross Rigg'. *Y.A.J.* 44 23-31. There is a model of the huts made by Rowland Close in the Ryedale Folk Museum.
48. Woodwark, Plate 12.
49. North Ings earthwork. Monastic enclosure Skelderskew. V.C.H. 2 p3
50. Brown, A.J. *Tramping in North Yorkshire*, Country Life, London, 1932 (p155).
51. EM, p148.
52. Yorks Inquisitions Post Mortem Surtees p48 13/14.
53. Four examples are known of paved trods continuing through cross passages of dwelling houses. See ref. 52 above.
54. Elgee, F. *Romans in Cleveland*, published by author, Commondale, 1923, p21 56.Latham, R. Latin Word List
56. The boundary of Danby & Glaisdale went through the cross-passage of Greenhouses below Tranmire (Inf. from Barry Harrison).
57. On R.A.F. photo 3550 taken 27.8.46.
58. Inman, R; Brown, D.R; Goddard, R.E and Spratt, D.A. 'Roxby Iron Age Settlement and The Iron Age in North East Yorkshire', *Proceedings of the Prehistoric Society* 51, 1985, pp181-213.
59. Sewell, p 25.
60. Mrs M Nattrass, 'Witch Posts and Early Dwellings in Cleveland', *Y.A.J. 34.* p 136-43.
61. Moore, RF *Paddy Waddell's Railway*, Whitby Literary and Philosophical Society, 1973. Revised and republished by North York Moors National Park Department, Helmsley, 1986.
62. *WNR Report p26-27, 1946-47*
63. Atkinson, JC *Gentleman's Magazine*, 1864, p17.
64. Forty Years p40.
65. Forty Years p85-6.
66. Westonby or Westinby. Yorks Inquests. Robt. de Schelton, held 1 carucate in the town of Westingby and renders yearly one pair of gloves.
67. Cucket Park - see Rimington, FC 'The Early Deer Parks of NE Yorks' pt II (catalogue) *SDAS Vol 2* no 15 p 35-37, 1972.
68. Young, p754
69. Excavated March 1966 by A Ridolls, W V Coles & R H Hayes at NZ 845100 in Skelder Plantation. No report published.
70. By R.H. Hayes in 1939.
71. Graves, Rev. J. *History of Cleveland*, Carlisle, 1808, p303 and also Young Vol. II, p726.
72. Ward, William G. *WNR* 1940, p25-30. An account of Egton including a photograph of the market hall taken about 1880.
73. Wade's Causeway, Fig 10, p79
74. Hayes, R.H. 'Romano-British Site NW of Newbiggin Hall' *YAJ 166 p120-25. 1962.*
75. Sewell, p26.
76. *Wade's Causeway*, p79-80, and Fig. 10, nos. 10, 11, 12, 13.
77. Sewell, p22.
78. *Report of Whitby Lit and Phil Soc*, 1980.
79. *North Riding Records*. Vol. VIII, 1711.
80. Young, Vol.2, p786.
81. *Wade's Causeway*, Fig 9, p27
82. *Whitby Nats Report no.5*, 1940-41, p48.
83. *Whitby Nats Rep Vol I* 1939-40. p3(Fred Wilkinson)
84. Sewell p16.
85. Sewell p16.

86. *Wades Causeway* p37-38 Map II
87. Elgee E.M. p205
88. *Goathland* Mrs Alice Hollins. Horne & Sons, Whitby, p15.
89. Sewell p17-18.
90. Rushton, J *The Ryedale Story*, Ryedale District Council, Malton, 1977. p32.
91. Foster Howes. Fosters were overseers under the Foresters in Fee according to Sewell p37 Appendix E.
92. Woodwark no. 4, p19 - Also known as John or Jack Cross.
93. Sewell p15.
94. Sewell p2, 20
95. Young Vol II, p579
96. Ramm, H. The Parisi. Duckworth, 1978, p53.
97 Saltersgate Inn had a famous turf fire reputedly never out for over 100 years, though Chequers on the Hambleton Road claimed the same period.
98. Recent research on Little Howe claims the artifacts found there are over 200-250 years later than the time of Lilla. *Medieval Archaeology XXV*, p153-56. The cross is not at all like a Saxon type - possibly replaced several times.
99. Sewell, p36 (Appendix)
100. Ann's Cross (Woodwark no 5). He says it marked the right-hand turn for York, otherwise the traveller would be in a bog. Has the shaft been broken near the arms?
101. Sewell,p38.
102. It is remarkable that there are three churches recorded at Hackness in Domesday Book (1086). St. Peter's still in use; St. Mary's (monastic church?) said to be under lake. The third could be the chapel of ease at Harwood Dale or the site on the 'chapel field' near Burgate. See Y.A.J. pt 108 p402-3, 1924 and F. C. Rimington, *SDAS 26*, p 3-10, 1988.
103. Woodwark, p13.
104. *North Riding Records*, Vol. II (New Series), op. 13.
105. H & H.
106. Atkinson, J. MOW, p182 and 324.
107. Hemingway, J.E. and Owen J. 'William Smith and the Jurassic Coals of Yorkshire', *Proc. of the Yorkshire Geological Soc.*, 1975, p302.
108. Woodwark, no.2.
109. Young, p 22 and Sewell p15.
110. Young, p443; F.C. Rimington, *SDAS 17*, p9-11, 1974.
111. *Wade's Causeway* p62-3.
112. *Wade's Causeway* p15
113. *Wade's Causeway* p69-75& B R Hartley SDAS no 21 p31-32 fig. 1978.
114. Goathland (ref 83) p70.
115. Hornsby W & Laverick JD 'The Roman Signal Station at Goldsborough near Whitby'. *Arch Journal Vol LXXXIX* 1932, p89.
116. Ashby, and Ap Simon, AP'Barnby Howes'. *Y.A.J.* 1956 p9-31.
117. *Wade's Causeway* p77.
118. Hildyard E J W & Hill P V,' A radiate Currency Hoard from Yorks.' *Numismatic Chronicle 18*, 1958.
119. Aberg, F.A. and Crossley, D.W. 'Hutton & Rosedale post medieval Glass Furnaces' *Post Medieval Archaeology Vol 6* 1972.
120. Hayes, R H & Hemingway J E,'The Glass Holes of Spaunton Moor' *Ryedale Historian* 12 p5-11, figs. 1984.
121. *Rosedale Mines and Railway* (ref 13) plate XXIV.
122. This is very similar to the legend of Wade's Wife laying the Roman causeway with stones carried in her apron. Wade's Causeway p16-17.
123. Clay, CT 'The Stuteville Fee'. *Early Yorkshire Charters*, Vol. IX, YAS Record Series, 1952.

124. Sewell, p23.
125. Also described by Joe Ford (see note 19) and Moore, R.F. *Lime roads in The Whitby District*, Whitby Lit. & Phil. Horne & Son, Whitby, 1972.
126. Cruck Buildings p39 (Fig 14).
127. Cruck Buildings, p93 and Fig 41.
128. Cruck Buildings, p93.
129. Forty Years, p56-8.
130. Pottery excavated by Smith and Gray in 1948-49 and now in Whitby Museum.
131. See Rimington, FC, p36-37 (as ref 63).
132. Correspondence with the writer in 1963.
133. Atkinson, J.C. (ed) 'Rievaulx Chartulary', *Surtees Society*, Vol 83, 1889, p176-7. Discussed in Helmsley p.72-3.
134. Thomas Parker, (1812-1902). Thatcher, poet and antiquarian from Wombleton, near Kirkbymoorside, whose unpublished notes of 1858 are in the RFM.
135. G. Jones,'The Cultural Landscape of Yorkshire: origins of our villages'. *Yorks. Phil. Soc. 1966*, p48.
136. RAF reference 4139, flown 14 April 1946.
137. Helmsley p345-6 fig 2 1-7.
138. Helmsley p207-8, 211-3.
139. Elgee, EM, p110.
140. Helmsley p374-5 and 378-9.
141. Hayes R H & Hemingway J E, 'Late 18th Century Coal Workings at Baysdale Head', *Ryedale Historian No 13*, 1986, p62.
142. Turton p 112-114.
143. Turton p43
144. Helmsley p73-4.
145. Atkinson (as ref 126), p179.
146. Helmsley, p431.
147. Turton p81.
148. Helmsley p122.
149. McDonnell, J. 'Medieval Assarting Hamlets in Bilsdale, *NE Yorkshire*', *Northern History, Vol XXII*, 1986, p269-79.
150. Whitaker A H. 'Coal Mining in Bransdale and Farndale in the Eighteenth Century'. *Ryedale Historian No. 4,* 1969, p55 - 63.
151. This cairn is called Obtrush Roque by the OS but the local name is Hobtrusch Rook - "the Hob goblin's Heap". John Phillips describes the rather rough excavation of it in 1836 by a large party of country folk-all they found was an empty cist. Phillips J., *Rivers, Moorland & Sea Coast of Yorks*, 1853, p210.
152. RAF reference 4138, flown 30 July 1951.
153. Helmsley, p211-219.
154. Forty Years, p219
155. *Rievaulx Charters*, p178 and Helmsley p69.
156. Bonser, K.J. *'The Drovers'*, MacMillan London,1970.
157. .Elgee E M p162; also Hayes RH 'The Hambleton Street', *SDAS I*, p21-29, 1960.
158. Spratt D A, 'Cleave Dike' *Y.A.J. 54* p49 1982.
159. Young, A. *Rural Economy of Yorkshire*, 1771, p51.
160. Bogg, Edmund. *Richmondshire and the Vale of Mowbray* E Stock (London) and J Miles (Leeds), 1906, p33.
161. Elgee E M, p47 & in Helmsley p12 plate IIa.
162. Spratt (ref 151) p36-39.
163. *YAS*. Record Series Vol 67 p157, 1246 AD.

164. Spratt, D.A. (ed) Prehistoric and Roman Archaeology in *NE Yorkshire BAR Series 104*, 1983, p198, fig 58.
165. Denny, H 'Notice of Early British Tumuli, Hambleton Hills'. Procs. of Yorks. *Geological & Polytechnic Society*, Vol iv, 1865. Referred to in Elgee, E M, p 240.
166. Helmsley, p458.
167. Helmsley p431. Perambulation of the Honour of Helmsley 1642. Now at North Yorkshire County Record Office, Northallerton.
168. Beresford, MW. *New Towns of the Middle Ages*, 1967.
169. VCH, Vol II, p332 (under Danby). The writer is quoting from an account in *The Archaeological Journal LIX*, p314-5.
170. Rolls of The North Riding Sessions, 1633.
171. Woodwark, no 10, p27-9.
172. The wrong picture is printed in Woodwark, 1970 as no 11. Swarth Howe Cross is shown. Woodwark says that White Cross is modern and the upper portion of the old cross is in Whitby Museum.
173. Elgee, E.M. p220-22, fig 67.
174. Part of this earthwork may have eroded near the edge; a sherd of 12th C pottery was found in ploughing on the west side.
175. Sewell, p23.
176. Rievaulx Charters of 1170 AD, p179.
177. f. 109 v & 109 r, 1007 AD.
178. Helmsley, p70.
179. Atkinson, *'Rievaulx Chartulary'*, (ref 126) p16-21, and p79 (1160 AD). Also Helmsley, p70.
180. Rievaulx Charters of 1333, p291-3, translated by B Harrison (unpublished).
181. Cooper I. *Helmsley 100 Years Ago*, York 1887, p19.
182. *Early Yorkshire Charters*, Vol IX, p665.
183. Keld Head chapel site Exc. by Miss G Fox, *Y.A.J.* 1939 p40.
184. Jeffrey R. *Thornton Dale*, 1930, p92.
185. Sewell, p33.
186. Rimington F C & Rutter J G, Ayton Castle, *S.D.A.S.* Rep 5 1967.
187. Jeffrey R. *Thornton Dale*, 1930. p41.
188. B M Coll. C7 DXI f 116r.
189. Hayes, R.H. 'Excavations at Spaunton Manor', *Ryedale Historian no 13*, 1986, p4-26.
190. Allison, M. 'An early Medieval Community near Appleton le Moors'. *SDAS no 23* p12-20, 1980.
191. Allison, M. 'The Medieval Free Chapel of Appleton le Moors', *Ryedale Historian, No. 13*, 1986. p52-54.
192. Whitaker, A.H. 'Excavation of a Roman aisled house near Spaunton' *Ryedale Historian 3*, 1967, p.61.
193. Air photos flown by RAF, 13 May 1950.
194. Hayes R H & Formstone G, A Romano-British site near Sinnington Manor. *SDAS* 20, 1980 (p 23-27) Figs 1-3.
195. Information from the late R W Crosland.
196. Sewell, p32.
197. Young, Vol I, p25,
198. Helmsley, p74.
199. Jervoise E. Ancient Bridges in The North of England, *SPAB, 1931, p67.*
200. *Wade's Causeway*, p20 and Map 3 (p21).
201. McDonnell, J 'The Bridge on Sinnington Green' *Ryedale Historian 2*, 1966, p50.
202. Forty Years, p443.
203. *Wade's Causeway,* p77-78.
204. Young, Vol II, p543.

205. In British Library, Egerton 2823, folio 109v.
206. Parratt, T W. 'Northern roads in The Middle Ages'. *Ryedale Historian No. 5* 1970; p.3 - 11. He quotes from the *North Riding Records, Vol IV*, New Series.
207. Hartley and Ingleby (ref 20), p106.
208. Sewell, p37, from *North Riding Records,* Vol IV, fo.194.
209. Sewell, p30.
210. Waites B. 'Medieval Fairs and Markets in North-East Yorkshire' *Ryedale Historian 1982*, p3.
211. Rushton, J. 'Life in Ryedale in the 14th Century' *Ryedale Historian* Pt 1, No. 8, 1976; Pt2, No 9, 1978.
212. Rutter, J G, 'Industrial Archaeology in North-East Yorkshire'. *SDAS 12 - 14*, 1969-71.
213. Young, p810.
214. White, W. *A Month in Yorkshire*, Chapman & Hall, London 1858.
215. Chapman, C *'Gazetteer of Cleveland Ironstone Mines'*, Langbaurgh Museum Service Research Series no. 1, 1975.
216. Hayes, RH. 'List of Early Iron-Working Sites in North-East Yorkshire', *Journal of the Historical Metallurgy Society* 12/1, 1978, ed Dr. R F Tylecote. Also see Helmsley, p458-60.
217. Owen, J S Paper on 'Jet' *Cleveland Industrial Archaeology no3*, 1975, p13-22.
218. Young, p817-8.
219. Sewell, p21, quoting from North Riding Records, Vol. VIII, fo.261.
220. Burnett, P 'Glaisdale Head Inscriptions', *WNR Report, Vol. 10*, 1945-47, p32-33.
221. Sewell, p24.

Late references

222. Edwards, *'The Early History of the North Riding'*, 1924, p199.
223. Rimington, F.C. 'The History of Ravenscar and Staintondale', *SDAS, 1988*.
224. Rimington, F.C. 'Foulbridge and its Preceptory' *SDAS 26*, 1988.
225. Brooke, D. "The Beacons of N. E. Yorkshire, *Ryedale Historian 14*, 1988-89.